THE DISCIPLE'S JOY

THE DISCIPLE'S JOY
six practices for spiritual growth

Michael W. Foss

Augsburg Books
MINNEAPOLIS

THE DISCIPLE'S JOY
Six Practices for Spiritual Growth

Cover design by Kevin van der Leek
Cover photo © Gansovsky Vladislay/iStock. Used by permission.

Library of Congress Cataloging-in-Publication Data
Foss, Michael W., 1948-
The disciple's joy : six practices for spiritual growth / Michael W. Foss.
p. cm.
ISBN 978-0-8066-5367-9 (alk. paper)
1. Christian life—Lutheran authors. 2. Joy—Religious aspects—Christianity. I. Title.
BV4647.J68F67 2007
248.4'841—dc22
2007022251

The paper used in this publication meets the minimum requirements of American National Standard for Information Sciences—Permanence of Paper for Printed Library Materials, ANSI Z329.48-1984.

Manufactured in the U.S.A.

10   09   08   07   2   3   4   5   6   7   8   9   10

For
Emme, Ethan, Olin and "The-Bix"
—the unborn grandchild I wait to meet in July—
They are gifts of God and sources of great joy to me.

May God be praised!

Contents

Acknowledgments

Any work is the result of the efforts of many—not just one. This book is no exception. I have benefited from some of the finest teachers, not only professors in college and seminary but the people of the congregations I have been privileged to serve. They have demonstrated a *real faith for real life* time and time again, often in unexpected ways and times. Some of their stories are in this book. All of them are in God's book of life.

I especially want to thank my three primary readers. They helped me find better ways to express my ideas and convictions. The first is my wife, Christine, who patiently read and listened to help me clarify my thoughts. The second is Julie Klein who served as my administrative assistant at Prince of Peace and who heard many of these stories and ideas before they found ink and paper. My third reader is the Chief of Staff at Lutheran Church of the Redeemer, Susan Cordell, who generously shared her time and ideas in improving the text. Any shortcomings in this work are mine alone but there would have been many more without the three of you and your help. Thank you.

Lastly, I want to acknowledge my pleasure at working once again with a fine editor, Henry French. It is rare to have someone who can "think your thoughts" naturally and, on occasion, better than you can. Hank has once again done that.

Preface

"Would you pray for my children?" he asked. We had gathered in Philadelphia for a conference and, after being paired up, were asked to share a prayer need and then pray for one another. This man, a member of a Lutheran praise band, and I had come together and now were sharing our prayer needs. That's when he asked me if I would be willing to pray with him about his family.

"What I really want you to pray for, pastor," he continued, "is that my children would find the same joy in Jesus Christ that I have found. I came to church after years of drug addiction and with a family that was falling apart. The church introduced me to the life of faith and I found joy. The truth is, pastor," he leaned in close, "most people in the church just don't know what they've got."

I reflected on my own experience apart from the Christian Church. I also had wandered but, by God's grace, was brought back to the church. The woman who helped me get back into the church also invited me into an adult Bible Study (a small group), and I haven't left the church since. It is my home, a place of real joy.

My experience is the same as that wonderful brother's in Pennsylvania. While we both admire the lives of those who have never lived apart from a Christian congregation, we have both seen that those who have stayed within the Church often don't really know what they've got.

That prayer, along with the realization that we both shared on that afternoon in Philadelphia, led to the dream of this book.

The Christian congregation is the primary point of contact between the loving God revealed in Jesus Christ and our world. This is where real people meet a real Savior who promises real joy.

I am not naive. Neither that Christian layman in Philadelphia nor I are unaware of the failings of the local church. Both of us have had enough experience in the church to recognize the politics as well as the propensity for pettiness, gossip, and blaming that is often present. But in the midst of all our human messiness, the Holy Spirit is at work.

The beating heart of the church is a shared faith that provides purpose, confidence, and an inner source of strength and serenity that external circumstances cannot dislodge for long. That's why the Christian Church, in its many forms, has proven so resilient over time.

I believe, as did my friend in Philadelphia, that the time has once again come to declare this central truth of our faith: God calls us—each one of us—to joy in Jesus Christ. In this book we will explore together the things that make for joy.

Chapter one asserts the God-given value of each human being, not for what we might become or what we could accomplish but simply for who we are. The creator God has endowed each person with infinite and eternal value. The coming of the incarnate Savior is the ultimate affirmation of this value.

Yet many of us, both in the church and outside of it, believe that we will be acceptable to God only when and if we become something we are not. We have a hard time accepting the fact that God loves us as we are. The invitation to joy is found first in God's radical love. But it doesn't stop there.

Joy deepens when we accept Christ's invitation to the journey of faith, a journey in which, by the power of God's

Holy Spirit, we are opened more and more to the gift of who we are in God. The New Testament contention is that we discover the breadth and depth of who we really are only when we trust God and walk boldly into the future God is already fashioning for us.

We take Jesus seriously when we claim his promise that a life with him is a life of abundance. Then we dare to live into that abundant life—and discover the best of ourselves in the process.

Chapter two argues that God desires us to experience lives of significance and purpose by aligning ourselves with the purposes of God. Purpose and significance will look different for different people because we are different. We are differently gifted and find ourselves in different situations and circumstances. Our significance and personal purpose emerge as we claim our unique gifts and match them with the opportunities for service that each of us receives from God.

Many within Christ's Church imagine that the purpose of God for them should be driven by a single over-riding passion that will inevitably lead to a radical change of life. This is not normally the case. We can live lives of great purpose and significance when—in the course of our ordinary, everyday lives—we let God's call to love and justice focus our passions and abilities in service to others. It will change our lives and bring us joy. Should it happen that we experience a profound, radical life change as we give ourselves to the purposes of God, I suspect we will discover that such a change is simply the outward expression of our best inner selves. It is a case of becoming more of who we are and not becoming someone we are not. Be that as it may, God's call to each of us is to find real purpose in living as real people whose passions are focused by faith to meet real needs in the real world.

In chapter three we will look more closely at the relationship between purpose and passion. Purpose is not a single focus that once discovered determines the rest of our lives. Instead, purpose is an ever evolving discovery. Life's opportunities and possibilities are changing gifts from God that invite us into increasing depth as we age. Our passions, interests, and abilities at age thirty will not be what they were at age twenty, nor what they will be at age forty, fifty, sixty, or seventy. Nevertheless, no matter how old we are, or how our passions, interests, and abilities change over time, Gods' call to love and justice will always have something significant for us to do.

Passion is the energy within our purpose. Unleashing our passion requires an openness to God's call to be loving people in the small—and sometimes large—opportunities that show up before us. Our willingness to grasp such opportunities is the kindling for unleashing the fires of passion within us.

Passion always directs us, sooner or later, more deeply into life and relationships. Both passion and purpose are expressed in loving, creative relationship with the world God loves.

Chapter four is an invitation to begin specific biblical and historic practices for spiritual development. The *Marks of Discipleship* engage the follower of Jesus Christ in spiritual disciplines that deepen our relationship with God, grow confidence in the promises of the Savior, and open our lives to the daily transforming presence of the Holy Spirit. As we practice the *Marks of Discipleship*, the secular is made sacred. The mundane, we discover, clothes the miraculous.

The *Marks of Discipleship* are behaviors, not ideas. Only when we deliberately and consistently practice our faith will we experience the deep joy that Jesus makes available to everyone.

Chapter five discusses some of life's great lessons as learned within the context of the life of faith. Walking with Jesus Christ reveals to us what really matters. Whether it is the experience of achievement, of beauty and love, or of loss and gain, the Holy Spirit provides us an eternal perspective on our experience. This spiritual perspective looks beyond the immediate to find what lasts—and why it lasts. In chapter five, you will be invited to reflect on your life values; it is an invitation to stop merely breathing and truly live.

Chapter six will sum things up and challenge you to push through the interferences that we all meet when we begin to live into the joy that comes from "faith working through love" (Galatians 5:6). We will examine images of God that impede rather than empower discipleship and explore some of the unexamined assumptions that keep us from experiencing all that God has prepared for us.

Running through each chapter of this little book is a common theme: joy is the birthright of those who follow Jesus, a birthright to be claimed and lived in and shared.

Many years ago I heard a sermon in which the pastor summed things up with an interesting turn of phrase. I don't remember much about the sermon or who the pastor was but this stuck with me: "Christians ought to have long faces—not north and south, but east and west!" The kingdom of heaven is served best by joy-filled Christians who, rather than simply endure life, have learned through faith to treasure life.

After telling his followers that people would know they were his disciples if they had love for each other (John 13:35), and then teaching them about love, Jesus told them: "I have said these things to you so that my joy may be in you, and that your joy may be complete" (John

15:11). That's your birthright—the disciple's joy. May this book help you claim it.

May the Spirit of Christ bless your reading, empower your faith, and guide your life.

CHAPTER ONE

God Didn't Make You to Become Someone Else!

GOD CREATED YOU FOR JOY

Joy is not the same thing as being happy. Our experience of happiness is a mere echo of true joy. Being happy is a very temporary reaction to present life circumstances. Happiness is transitory—it arises and falls away as our circumstances change.

Joy, on the other hand, is foundational—it persists (and often deepens) through changing circumstances. Joy breaks through the realities of our present situation, reframes the present situation in the light of God's infinite grace and love, and enables us to live both trustingly and confidently through whatever circumstances life brings our way.

Unlike joy, happiness disappears in the face of pain. Yet the great lessons of life are almost always learned by reflecting on our personal experiences of discomfort or pain. People who confuse happiness with joy rarely learn these deep lessons of life. Their constant (and futile) pursuit of happiness as an end in itself precludes their pondering the lessons of pain.

Joy transforms our experiences of personal pain to purpose. Those who understand this and pursue joy find in their own sorrow and suffering a universal connection to life. Joy reframes pain by placing it within the context of a deeper life purpose. Joy integrates the present into a much larger vision of life as a whole.

Let me illustrate with a story:

"Hi, pastor," he said with a grin. "I'm so glad you came," and then with a glance at his watch, he continued, "and right on time too."

I had met him a couple of weeks earlier at church. His wife was disabled and, though she had once been very actively involved, was now bedridden at home. Their home was a small 50's style ranch house, modestly furnished. As I entered I noticed family pictures arranged on a buffet that overlooked polished wood floors and a colorful area rug. The warmth of his smile and handshake was reflected in the home that seemed to gently embrace me as I entered.

"She's over here on the sofa," he said. "She's asleep, but I'll wake her."

"I can come back another time, Walt," I offered.

"Of course not, she's expecting you," he said. Then he led me into their small living room and I looked down at a seemingly frail woman wrapped in a blanket, fast asleep. Walt looked down and simply said, "Isn't she beautiful?" His eyes danced as he looked at his wife of nearly fifty years. "Before her bones began to break, she was really something." He glanced at me. "She's lost about three inches off her height and suffers quite a bit when she tries to walk. But," he continued as he turned back to her, "when I look at her, I see the young woman I married."

Turning to me, he said, "You wouldn't know it now, but we used to dance together every Saturday night. She was so agile, and I'd see others watching us as we danced. We were quite a pair." Then he turned to smile at her once more.

Gently he reached down and touched her shoulder. "Marsha," he said softly, "Honey, wake up. The pastor is here."

She stirred. Then she awakened, saw him and smiled. "The pastor's here," he repeated and gestured toward me. Her eyes turned to me, she smiled—she was beautiful.

Joy is a deep well that can refresh us in the driest desert. Walt and Marsha shared joy. Even as they shared in her pain, their joy was transparent. And through the years I knew them, their joy never seemed far away—until the evening she died. His heart was broken. The light of his joy returned only weeks after the funeral when we spoke, and he could share his memories of their life together and talk about how he could feel good that she was no longer in pain.

> Faith takes our moments of both happiness and sorrow, collects them, and arranges them into a worldview that sees God's hand in all things. Therein is joy.

It has been my privilege to know countless people like Walt and Marsha, people whose circumstances could not be characterized as a cause for happiness. It never occurred to me to ask them if they were happy. Such a question was simply too petty. But over the years I began to understand that in spite of their circumstances they experienced a deep joy. Their joy transformed their suffering into moments that transcended the pain and affirmed all the pleasure, happiness, and achievements they had experienced and shared for years.

Only God can create and unlock such personal power. Joy is the spiritual energy that we commonly call the blessing of God. Faith is the conduit for this blessing. Faith opens the heart to receive the deepening agent of life that we call joy. Faith takes our moments of both happiness and sorrow, collects them, and arranges them into a worldview that sees God's hand in all things. Therein is joy.

LETTING GO OF FALSE UNDERSTANDINGS

How remarkable then that so many people have such a contrary picture of God and God's will for our lives! If you ask most people about God's will they will describe a God whose demands of us are anything but joyful. God is all too often seen as a stern parent who expects us to set aside the things we most would like to do. And the things that we enjoy the most always seem like forbidden fruit. Like a child who is forced to take piano lessons when he would rather be playing soccer, we are invited to church with the reprimand, "Someday you'll thank me for this!" And just like that child, we simply cannot imagine it.

How different the witness of the Bible is, a witness reflected in the lives of so many wonderful people like Walt and Marsha!

Jesus Christ is God's invitation to joy, God's promise of joy. But we must first let go of our false understandings of what the Bible says and what God demands of us in order to receive this incredible promise. That is what growing faith does: challenges our false assumptions about God and Christianity.

For example: God didn't create you to make you become someone else! The witness of the Bible is that God's deepest desire is for each of us to become more fully who we are and all that we were created to be. "For we are what he has made us, created in Christ Jesus for good works, which God prepared beforehand to be our way of life" (Ephesians 2:10). In fact, only when we can accept this truth will we fully understand and live our divine purpose. Joy is lost to us in the frantic search for happiness when we cannot see God's hand in who we are, in our passions and interests, gifts and talents.

The psalmist celebrates this touch of eternity in our individual uniqueness in these profound words:

O Lord, you have searched me and known me. You
know when I sit down and when I rise up; you discern
my thoughts from far away. . . . For it was you who
formed my inward parts; you knit me together in my
mother's womb. I praise you, for I am fearfully and
wonderfully made. Wonderful are your works; that I
know very well. (Psalm 139:1-2, 13-14)

God is the author of our uniqueness! God celebrates
each of us in the wonderful particularity of our identities.
God desires joy for each of us and comes again and again to
meet us and bless
us with it. But we
cannot receive the
blessing if we are
not open to it. How

> To truly *trust* the God we meet
> in Jesus of Nazareth is to *fol-
> low* the God we meet in Jesus of
> Nazareth.

can we be open to this divine touch in our lives if we believe
it will come only at the cost of losing our identities?

Throughout the Gospels Jesus teaches that we are
eternal investments of God. God creates each of us for
a purpose unique to ourselves. This purpose is unlocked
when we can truly hear God's affirmation of who we are
and what we can become. But this is only possible through
the gift of faith. Faith is trusting God—the God we meet
in Jesus of Nazareth. To truly *trust* the God we meet in
Jesus of Nazareth is to *follow* the God we meet in Jesus of
Nazareth. Faith and following go hand in hand.

BEING WHO WE ARE

I grew up the second of four boys. My older brother was
my best friend when I was young and I admired him
greatly. He always seemed to me to be smarter and more
popular than I was. The brother just younger than me was
a star athlete. While I worked two jobs, he lettered in many

sports. My youngest brother was the cute one. He seemed so well adjusted and happy all the time. When I looked at my brothers, whom I love, I wasn't sure of my own place. So it came as a great shock to me that God would want me to simply be me. I can't remember how it happened. I know the realization grew over time. But there was one moment when, as I was driving a warehouse truck, I suddenly realized that I had a special place in the heart and will of God. I didn't have to try and be someone else. God was inviting me to grow into myself!

Many people both within and outside of the Church haven't grasped this incredible truth. Yet over and over again in the Gospels of the New Testament, we see the response of joy to Jesus' simple affirmation of an individual's worth in themselves. Just read the story of Zacchaeus (Luke 19:2), the parable of the prodigal son, (Luke 15:1), and every story of Jesus' healings of bodies, minds, and spirits.

The woman at the well was so taken by Christ's acceptance of her—even though he knew of her relationship failures—that she ran into the village to bring others to him. As a social outcast she knew what it felt like to have others expect her to be someone else, to dress up her act and get it right. The unexpected love of God erupted in joy within her and she went *just as she was* back to those who had rejected her to share with them what she had discovered in the presence and person of Jesus.

Walt and Marsha knew this joy. Their Saturday night dancing was not incongruous with their Sunday morning worship. They were created with the ability to dance, and when they danced together they praised the God who created them. When they worshiped they heard the very same affirmation that woman heard at a well so many centuries ago. Like the woman at the well, Walt and Marsha had come to see with God's eyes of love and faith; it unlocked joy within and between them.

Jesus said, "I came that they may have life, and have it abundantly" (John 10:10), which is to say that he came that we might have joy! And he wasn't kidding. He wasn't promising something that we would receive only when this life was over. He wasn't playing the "magical thinking" game and promising that we'd always be happy. Rather, he promised a deep satisfaction in living, a quiet confidence in life that can translate whatever happens to us into an experience that creates growth and richness of life. That is the treasure that Walt and Marsha would share with me over the months I knew them.

After visiting with them I would often ask myself how they could possibly be so happy. How was such joy possible when she was just a shadow of what she once was? How could he see a beautiful woman—and he truly did—in this woman who could hardly sit up without pain?

But I was observing their situation out of context. I saw their *situation* as the definition of who they were. They didn't. This was only a page in the wonderful book of love that they had written with their lives. God created them for joy—and they knew it. When I came to understand this, I began to see them as they saw each other and I began to see their situation as they did—a moment wrapped in the grace of God.

GIVING UP OUR PREOCCUPATION WITH THE IMMEDIATE

There is a cost for such joy as this. We must give up our preoccupation with the immediate.

"I'm just stuck," he said as he shook his head. "Ever since my wife's affair, our divorce, and the custody settlement, I can't seem to get past it. I know I should," he sighed, "but I just can't."

"Can you tell me what you see in your mind's eye when you think of being stuck?" I asked.

"Yes, I see her face." He stopped, then looked up and continued, "No, that's not right. What I see is my family altogether."

"Who do you see?" I asked.

"Well, I see myself and my children and. . . ." He began to frown. He closed his eyes. I waited in silence. "You know," he continued, "this is interesting. I see a woman there but there's no face." And looking up, he asked, "What does that mean?"

"I don't know," I replied. "What do you think it means?"

He thought for awhile and then said, "I think it means that I haven't forgiven my ex-wife for destroying my dream of the perfect family."

"Do you think that God won't give you another partner with whom you can rebuild your dream of a family?" I asked.

"But I failed. God hates divorce—I just know he does!" he said strongly. "I can't accept the fact that God would tolerate what has happened and just let me go on."

"So," I asked gently, "God forgives only partially? What about the thief on the cross? Did Jesus really mean it when he said, 'Today you'll be in paradise with me?' Or not? And if Jesus can give a new beginning to a convicted man, what about you?"

Begin to build your tomorrow on the fact of God's love for you today.

"So, what should I do?" he asked.

"Take God seriously," I replied. "Trust that no matter what you feel, God has forgiven you and desires that you rediscover joy in your life. If you go by what you feel you'll be trapped by whatever mood is upon you. And, frankly, what you have been through has led you into a time of grief and self-doubt—which is natural!"

"I'm suggesting that you put this season of personal struggle within the larger context of God's love and forgiveness. Then act *as if* you really believe that. Begin to build your tomorrow on the fact of God's love for you today. I'm not suggesting," I continued, "that you pretend your feelings don't exist. I am suggesting that you no longer give them power over you and your future."

The cost of our preoccupation with the immediate is our inability to experience today in the context of God's invitation to joy. By surrendering our preoccupation with the immediate and trusting in God, we move again towards joy. This is liberating, as our young man discovered. He went on to marry another. Divorce shattered his earlier dream of a perfect family, but his hopes for a life partner to love and be loved by, and who would share his love for his children, were wonderfully realized.

God does not ask us to place our current pain or sorrow in a greater context without promising us that it will be worth it. Before the man in our story could move into God's future for him he had to let go of both his anger towards his ex-wife and his self-castigation. His very natural feelings of guilt and grief tied his hands to the past by locking him in his unhappy present. Letting go of the past freed him from the self-imposed prison of his feelings. Later his feelings would catch up with his hopes and trust in God.

The same can be said for the need to set aside immediate pleasure. Temptation is the lure of the immediate at the expense of the truly worthwhile. For many this will seem like an entirely new way to understand temptation, but it isn't. When Jesus stared down the Devil in the desert

(Matthew 4:1-11), each temptation was an attempt to get him to squander his identity and calling for the sake of an immediate payoff. Jesus resists by placing each temptation within the greater context of God's good will.

Temptation is as much about our willingness to deny the best of ourselves as it is about our willfulness and self-assertion in the face of God's invitation to joy. If God created us for joy, then turning away from God is also turning away from God's desire that we be all that we were created to be.

What parents have not seen their children choose an immediate pleasure at the expense of what would most certainly bring greater joy? When this happens we often assume that it's a matter of immaturity. We console ourselves by assuring ourselves that life experience will help the child learn to choose the greater and not the lesser. This hope of the parent is for the sake of the child. We understand that self-restraint will often lead to a much better end than self-indulgence. Tragically, many adults seem not to have learned this crucial lesson.

GOD'S COMMANDMENTS AND JOY

With this in mind we can understand the commandments of God. God doesn't need them. We do. God's invitation to joy is embedded in the commandments, particularly in the Ten Commandments.

For many people the Ten Commandments are impositions or, at best, helpful guidelines for living. But something changes when we see them as divine instruments to grow joy within us. The first commandments remind us that joy is the consequence of faith: trusting God and living toward God's goal for our lives (love). The remaining commandments place our relationships within the greater context (love) that makes for joy.

Of course knowing this does not make the commandments easier to keep. Instead, it reorients our understanding of God and God's will for us. We no longer see God as a stern task master who would deny us pleasure and happiness. Rather, we come to see that the very nature of God is love and that what God wants both for us and from us is love. We should never forget that Jesus collapsed all the commandments into two: love God who made you and love your neighbor as yourself (Matthew 22:37-40).

LOVE AND JOY

Love desires what is best for the other—not one's own happiness or pleasure. When St. John declares that God is love (1 John 4:8, 16), he is declaring that God is self-giving will. Jesus, the will of God made flesh, demonstrated that God always seeks what is best for us through his willingness to give his very life for our sakes. On the night he was betrayed into the hands of those who would have him killed, Jesus taught his followers one last time about love. He declared that people would know they were his followers only if they loved each other in the same manner he loved them (John 13:35). He then told them, "I have said these things to you *so that my joy may be in you, and that your joy may be complete*" (John 15:11). God's love is the source of our joy. When we love we complete our joy. Without love there is no joy.

> We come to see that the very nature of God is love and that what God wants both for us and from us is love.

In our broken and sinful world we are, at best, people learning to love. Joy is, therefore, something that can only be grown over time and with great care. Few of us will discover deep joy apart from deep sorrow and loss. And we will not develop this spiritual depth without freely choosing to set aside the immediate for the long lasting, the temporary for the eternal, self-centeredness for other-centeredness. To borrow a phrase from St. Paul, "faith working through love" (Galatians 5:6) is the conduit of joy, the soil from which joy will spring.

Remember Walt and Marsha. They were human, as we all are, and we should not imagine that their relationship was perfect. Without doubt there were moments of anger and hurt, misunderstanding and emotional distance. It happens. But I know they were sustained by a shared joy rooted in the rich soil of their love for each other.

Such joy is planted as a seed of possibility in every human soul. It is cultivated by love—the love of God and that human love that finds its source in God. Such joy is not beyond any of us. Joy to see us through all the trying circumstances of life is within reach of each person uniquely created by the hand of God. The only question is whether we will strive to claim this divine intent for our lives by trusting God's love for us and then giving ourselves in and for love.

God created you and me for joy. Which is to say God created us for love. Discover yourself and claim God's will for you as the gift of grace it is. Let the will of God reframe your present situation into one of spiritual growth, learning and true joy. Trust that God is at work in you and through you for good—no matter what. Commit yourself to finding that good. Then watch as God grows joy deep within you over time.

QUESTIONS FOR FURTHER REFLECTION

❦ How would you explain the difference between "happiness" and "joy"? Give some examples of each from your own life experience.

❧ Do you think it is possible to have joy without love; that is, without God's love for us, and without our loving God, others, and ourselves? Why? Or why not?

❧ How does the faith that God wants us to grow into who we are invite us to discover joy?

❧ Does God's forgiveness create a new future? Why? Or why not?

❧ Do you think joy is possible in conflict and other difficult circumstances? How or how not?

❧ When have you experienced the simultaneity of love and joy?

CHAPTER TWO

The Power of Significance

I rang the doorbell and a voice called out, "Is that you, pastor?" I answered in the affirmative and the voice called again, "Well, come on in. I left the door open for you."

It was spring and wonderfully warm. I opened the screen door and entered into the small but well kept home. Marie was seated on an old wingback chair. She smiled and extended her hand.

"I hope you don't mind me not getting up," Marie said, "it's just that, with this bad hip it takes awhile and hurts like blazes. And, by the way, there's some fresh coffee in the kitchen, so, pastor, just help yourself."

I thanked her, got a cup of coffee for both of us, and then sat down and got to know this wonderfully optimistic lady.

Finally, I asked the question that kept coming back to me again and again during our 30 minute conversation. "Marie, I know you don't get out much," I began, "so how do you keep such a great attitude? You don't seem depressed even though you are housebound most of the time."

She smiled and said, "Oh, pastor, I have had such a full life. And it's not over." Her eyes twinkled. "You see, I pray. I pray every day for people and situations. I pray everyday for you and the church. And I have seen miracles grow from my prayers. It may not sound like much to some people, but I know that prayer changes things. So, I pray."

Significance is not solitary. Significance is relational. That doesn't mean that we cannot have a profound sense of personal, individual purpose. Having our lives matter is a critical need within every human being. But our lives cannot matter if they matter just to ourselves.

Significance is always in relationship to someone or something else. The joy to which our God invites us is our call to purpose, to living beyond ourselves in love.

Most of us exaggerate the call of God to significance. We believe that our significance must have great spiritual impact and be highly visible. In so doing, we minimize the ordinary miracle of God's call. God gives an invitation to significance to every person in every situation.

Marie didn't make God's call a matter of spiritual pride. She understood her call as a connection to both God and others for the purposes of God. The physical world had shrunk to the size of her small home with momentary excursions out. But her spiritual world was as big as her faith, her love, and her willingness to pray.

> The joy to which our God invites us is our call to purpose, to living beyond ourselves in love.

And pray she did. Prayer was her work and her life. Prayer was her lifeline to others. This connection to others proved so strong that it became a mutual sharing. I remember how startled I was when I learned that members of the congregation often called her and asked for prayers, pouring their life stories and needs out over the phone to a listener who became their advocate before God. Not surprisingly, I would also call her and ask for prayers. They were most frequently for others and their needs, but on a few occasions they were for me.

How effective were Marie's prayers? I don't know. How confident was I in her praying? Very confident. I knew without a doubt that she prayed with a spirit of confidence and joy.

It was her joy that was both startling and inspiring. After all, she had every reason to turn inward. She was a shut in with on-going relationships that had dwindled to only a few life long friends, or so it seemed. She lived with chronic pain from a hip problem.

> No one can ascribe significance to us. We must feel it, claim it, and commit to it.

Her personal mobility was severely limited; even if she wanted to drive she couldn't manage the hip pain she experienced from the simple task of moving her foot from accelerator to brake. She was dependent upon others to go anywhere. Yet, she had discovered joy.

Or should I say that joy had discovered her? I don't know when Marie experienced the call to prayer ministry. What was obvious, however, was that her sense of purpose and personal fulfillment grew from that call.

That's the other side of significance. Significance may be relational—to a higher purpose and to relationship with others—but it is ultimately personal. No one can ascribe significance to us. We must feel it, claim it, commit to it and realize it.

Joy, as I have previously mentioned, is different from being happy because it grows from within us and is not dependent upon our external circumstances. Joy comes upon us and we are surprised—just like Marie had been surprised by what prayer had come to mean in her life and, through her, in the lives of so many others. She had no pretense to being spiritually superior or special. She just knew that prayer "changed things." I never asked her, but I am confident that she knew the first thing prayer changed was her.

Having been surprised by this call to prayer, Marie then claimed it for herself. I believe that each of us is called, again and again, to significance in life. But since the call often doesn't come in a dramatic form, we dismiss it. Those who have discovered joy and the call to significance, however, follow through and begin to live the call—in the ordinariness of their everyday lives.

That's exactly what Marie did and continued to do. Her acceptance of God's call to a significant life of prayer led to a continuing commitment to pray for all those God placed in her way. This daily commitment to prayer led her to a deeper relationship with her Savior, Jesus, as well as to profound relationships (grounded in love) with those for whom she prayed. Hers was a deeply significant and joyful life.

> God's call will be shaped by who we are, what we are capable of, and what the circumstances of our lives will allow.

Joy deepens within us when we claim and commit ourselves to the particular invitations to significance that God calls us to throughout the seasons of our lives. For most of us God's call to significance will change—perhaps many times—over the course of our lives. God's call will be shaped by who we are, what we are capable of, and what the circumstances of our lives will allow.

Here, in the winter of her life, Marie's call to significance was not to adopt orphaned children nor was it to lead women's Bible studies. Instead, it was the simple call to prayer—a call that fit and enriched her life circumstances. Her call to significance transformed her small living room into a ministry that reached far beyond the limits of our small town.

> Once while Jesus was standing beside the lake of Gennesaret, and the crowd was pressing in on him to hear the word of God, he saw two boats there at the shore of the lake; the fishermen had gone out of them

and were washing their nets. He got into one of the boats, the one belonging to Simon, and asked him to put out a little way from the shore. Then he sat down and taught the crowds from the boat. When he had finished speaking, he said to Simon, "Put out into the deep water and let down your nets for a catch." Simon answered, "Master, we have worked all night long but have caught nothing. Yet if you say so, I will let down the nets." When they had done this, they caught so many fish that their nets were beginning to break. So they signaled their partners in the other boat to come and help them. And they came and filled both boats, so that they began to sink. But when Simon Peter saw it, he fell down at Jesus' knees, saying, "Go away from me, Lord, for I am a sinful man!" . . . Then Jesus said to Simon, "Do not be afraid; from now on you will be catching people." When they had brought their boats to shore, they left everything and followed him. (Luke 5:1-11)

I have always found it fascinating where Jesus found his disciples. They weren't in the synagogue. They were not in a prayer meeting. They were ordinary people who heard the call of God in their ordinary lives. Having been found by joy, they claimed the call and committed to it. Their following of the Messiah grew out of their experience of God in the mundane chores of life, the God who can make miracles out of our everyday activities. By accepting and committing to God's call to significance, they were invited into a lifelong walk with the joy-giver, Jesus.

SOMETIMES GOD HAS A DIFFERENT IDEA
"Pastor Mike, I don't know what's happening in my life," she said.

"What do you mean?" I asked.

She was a young Christian, having given her life to Jesus Christ at the ripe old age of 40. She worshiped with us as often as her job would allow, and that wasn't every Sunday. As a single mom her job as a cashier at a local grocery store was essential for providing for her family and she had to work when scheduled. So when she signed up to learn and practice the *Marks of Discipleship* (see chapter four), she was worried about her inability to worship every week. I explained to her that she could easily get CDs of our Sunday worship and then take time for worship later in the week when she had to work on Sunday.

Now she had stopped to chat with me after church.

"I don't know what's happening but people are stopping at my cash register and, while paying for their groceries, they tell me things about their lives that are really private. And I listen and then tell them I'll pray for them. When I see them the next time, I quietly ask if things are better—and they tell me! What's going on? They keep coming back, waiting in my line even if it's longer than the other lines just to talk with me."

I smiled. "I think that they just know, on a spiritual level, that you will listen and care. It sounds to me like God is transforming your cash register into a mission field."

She thought about it and replied, "Well, that makes sense." Then she laughed, "I guess when I became a Christian I thought it would just remain between me, the Lord, and the church—but it seems God has a different idea."

God often has a different idea. We don't know how many people were called to follow Jesus and then were sent back to live out that call in the ordinariness of their usual lives, but I suspect there were many.

When Jesus called Peter and his fellow fishermen to follow him, he didn't use deep theological or spiritual language.

Instead, he brought significance into their ordinary lives using language that fit their ordinary lives: "Do not be afraid; from now on you will be catching people." I suspect that whenever Simon went fishing after that, as he doubtless did, he always thought of that day, and the great catch of fish, and the many people he would draw into the net of God's love and grace.

My friend did not return to her cash register at the local grocery store with the same old attitude. Her life situation had changed through faith. Now her perspective on her work had changed to fit this new soul understanding of life and others. Instead of a mere job, she came to understand her work as a ministry of love. Instead of mere customers, she saw the people in her checkout line as God's beloved people in need. This subtle shift in attitude brought with it a sense of significance that was transforming for her.

I don't know if she is still at that grocery store as a cashier or not. It is possible that her new understanding opened her to a new vocation. But it doesn't always. Instead, her sense of purpose, like that of Marie, could have invited her into a future of joy right where she was. In any case her life had been touched by a miracle of grace— just like Simon Peter and his companions.

But notice again how her invitation to significance connected her to others. When God calls, "faith working through love" is not far behind. She simply needed to reframe her work experience in the light of God's love and God's call to love. I was able to help her reframe her experience in such a way *Joy is expecting to meet God in this day.* that she was empowered to claim and commit to the God-given purpose growing within and through her by faith.

Leaving everything to follow Jesus did not mean physically leaving what she was doing, as it did for Simon Peter and the others. Instead, it meant letting go of how she understood what she was doing. She had to leave behind her small ideas of faith and her limited perception of the spiritual possibilities of her life. On the other side of her limited present was a future of joy in a ministry that she had never considered before.

Leave taking is necessary for joy. Joy cannot be found in yesterday's frustration over fruitless labor nor in a mechanical washing of nets in the hope of tomorrow's catch. Joy isn't found in passively accepting our personal situations any more than in narrowly defining our work lives in terms of hours worked and wages earned.

Joy is expecting to meet God in this day.

No one expects to meet another without some preparation. How shall we prepare to meet the God of joy? Leave taking is the spiritual preparation that we need to meet God today—and there is *no other time* to meet God than today. Joy is about choosing to live today—not yesterday nor tomorrow, but this one day.

First, we must take our leave of yesterday. I am not suggesting that we no longer remember our past. Memory is a gift from God when appropriately used. Memory aids us in our life long journey of learning. We remember and we can apply yesterday's lessons to today's problems or opportunities. We remember and we are not naive in relationships nor are we grandiose in imagining our own possibilities. Memory speaks of lessons learned and limitations owned. As such, memory can be an aid in preparing to meet the God of joy.

TAKING LEAVE OF YESTERDAY

Leave taking of yesterday relegates our past to the past. We choose not to live any longer in the past. The hurts and resentments that build up in any life will, over time,

THE POWER OF SIGNIFICANCE

block our experience of joy. Even past glories can dim today's joy for us. Living in the past makes today a mere shadow of yesterday. Whatever happens today is either infected by our past or overshadowed by it.

I have never forgotten a visit with a woman who spent our time together telling me of the husband she had lost. I listened and my heart ached for her. This was a wonderful man who had touched her life with love. No wonder she missed him. Her description of him brought him to life in my imagination and I told her I wished I had known him. After we prayed, I left glad that I had been able to connect with this wonderful, recently (I thought) widowed woman.

> If you would have joy, take leave of yesterday. Let the emotional power of yesterday belong to yesterday.

Imagine my surprise when I learned that she had lost her husband nearly 20 years before my visit! Because she still lived in her loss, her grief was as ragged that day as it had been the first few weeks after his death. She couldn't embrace her life because she was stuck in the shadow of yesterday. Later I learned that she was a source of great concern for those who loved her because they could see that she was just going through the motions of life. Today had no promise because yesterday had brought death to her husband.

I have seen resentments from the past curdle the love of the present. I have watched as the failures of yesterday's relationships have doomed people to either loneliness or frantic clinging in the here and now.

I had been invited and had agreed to do their wedding, so we met in my office. As we chatted, this middle aged couple seemed charming and genuinely in love. In the course of the conversation, I learned that they had gone through pre-marital counseling in another state and that each had been married before. Somewhere in the conversation I asked if they talked with one another about their previous marriages and what went wrong. Shaking his head, he declared strongly, "We have never talked about them—and we won't! That just brings old failures back to life and we are beginning new with each other." And she agreed.

I was not surprised that the marriage lasted less than a year. Their unspoken past was too great a burden for the hoped for tomorrow or the lived in today. Their relationship was filled with the ghosts of past hurts and betrayals. The problem with yesterday's resentments is that they are like a hole in the pocket. Not only do we lose valuable things through them—like joy and love—but, not dealt with, they always get larger and the larger they get the more we lose.

If you would have joy, take leave of yesterday. Let the emotional power of yesterday belong to yesterday. How? First, freely acknowledge and own the events of the past. When appropriate, discuss them with those whom you trust and, if needed, with others whose lives may have been impacted by them. Then, refuse to spend the time or energy on them that they often demand. The truth is that the past is best remembered—not revered or relived.

THE POWER OF FORGIVENESS

Practicing forgiveness is one way to prepare to meet God in the present. Forgiveness will help to lessen the power of yesterday over your life. But forgiveness is not well understood by many people both inside and outside the Christian church.

Forgiveness is a three step process that is necessary when another person has sinned against us or done something wrong to us. Forgiveness doesn't pretend that everything is alright. It assumes, in fact, that the opposite is true. Christian forgiveness is, therefore, not naive. We take seriously both the reality of our pain and the gravity of the other's actions when we choose to forgive. When we forgive we are choosing to no longer allow others to have power over us through the actions they have taken against us. We are also choosing to live in the purpose God calls us to today rather than in yesterday's hurts and resentments.

The first step in the process of forgiveness is to deliberately *decide* to forgive. This is an exercise of the will. We consciously decide that we will act *as if* the sin was behind us. Then we discipline ourselves to live into this decision.

Thus the second step in forgiving is choosing to act in accordance with our decision to forgive. We don't pretend that what happened didn't occur, but we give up any desire for revenge and we act as civilly as we reasonably can with those who have hurt us. St. Paul's advice is as good today as it was when he first gave it: "Do not repay anyone evil for evil, but take thought for what is noble in the sight of all. If it is possible, so far as it depends on you, live peaceably with all. Beloved, never avenge yourselves. . . . Do not be overcome by evil, but overcome evil with good" (Romans 12:17-19, 21).

Although genuine forgiveness may lead to restoring a broken relationship, in some cases it may not, and perhaps should not. In abusive, violent relationships, for example, we may justifiably choose not to pursue a renewed relationship, but we must reject any thoughts When we truly forgive another person it *may* transform them; of revenge and it *will* transform us. leave the one who hurt us to the judgment of God. Indeed, to truly forgive someone who has deeply hurt us is to pray that they would come to experience all the goodness God desires for them.

The last step in the process of forgiveness is choosing to move ahead despite our feelings of hurt, anger, or resentment. Many make the mistake of thinking that they cannot forgive until they "feel" like forgiving, but remember: forgiveness is an act of the will. We forgive because (often in spite of our feelings) we choose to forgive. We choose to free ourselves from yesterday and the power of past hurts. We choose to get on with our lives in the here and now by focusing on God's good intentions for us and not on the bad intentions of others.

Forgiveness is the first step in our own healing. When we truly forgive another person it may transform them; it *will* transform us.

The decision to forgive may need to be made again and again. No matter how spiritually mature we judge ourselves to be, letting go of the past and its hurts is not easy. Just as we daily claim and commit to joy, so must we daily forgive in order to be finally free for today.

It is not too much to say that with our deepest hurts and disappointments, the most profound of our betrayals, forgiveness is about us. We choose joy; we choose not to live under the oppressive burden of yesterday's hurts and yesterday's negative feelings. But let me repeat, forgiveness does not mean that we naively reenter into relationships that have wounded us in the past. The abused spouse forgives so that he or she can be free for a healthy relationship *with someone else*.

Without forgiveness our own wisdom is clouded over and we are likely to blindly engage in a vicious cycle where we are hurt by others, where we hurt ourselves, and where we hurt others over and over again. Forgiveness declares an end to this cycle of hurt by opening us to our own healing while we entrust the abusive other to God—and leave them to find their own way to healing.

QUESTIONING UNQUESTIONED ASSUMPTIONS

So much of what we do today is shaped and guided by old (and usually unquestioned) assumptions from the past that are no longer (if they ever were) adequate to today's realities. Choosing to find joy by living into today also means, therefore, examining and going beyond those old assumptions of the past.

Margaret Blanchard, of the Blanchard Organization, tells of the time when she was asked by the management team to become the organization's futurist. Concerned to continue meeting the needs of a fast paced and deeply changing world of business, they believed they needed someone to help them anticipate the future with all of its changes. Ms. Blanchard told us that she accepted immediately and, after delegating her responsibilities to others, she began thinking about the future.

After a few months she returned to the management team and declared that she suffered from "educated incapacity." She knew so much about the past and the present that she didn't have any mental room to learn about the future. She had to *unlearn what she knew in order to learn what she needed to know.*

She was right. In order to let go of yesterday and live with joy in God's present, we must be willing to unlearn past assumptions and conclusions in order to learn what we need to know to live as God would have us live today. This doesn't mean forgetting all we have learned. It does mean that in order to fully embrace today we must test yesterday's learning. Much of it will stand the test of today; some of it will not.

If we cling to yesterday's assumptions as unquestioned truth for today, we turn away from the God who makes the present new and, in doing so, opens a new future to us. Unless those fishermen were willing to let go of yesterday's learning (there was no fish out there!) they would not have been open to Jesus' advice and the great miracle that followed. Unless the woman at the grocery checkout line was willing to let go of yesterday's assumptions about her work she would never have come to see her cash register as a place of ministry where her caring faith intersected the lives of so many others in need.

> We live into today by asking, "What do I need to unlearn today in order to learn what God would have me know?"

We live into today by asking, "What do I need to unlearn today in order to learn what God would have me know?"

KEEPING THE PAST THE PAST

A healthy past is a remembered past, not a revered past. The memory of yesterday in a healthy life is the foundation for engaging today with all of its surprises and learning. A healthy attitude to our past (achieved through forgiveness and letting go) opens us to joy because it opens us to this one day: today.

But what about those who live in past glories? Their experience of today is often the empty and false echo of yesterday's achievements.

Some years ago I served in a community where many of the leaders had been "stars" in their high school. Some had been athletes, others cheerleaders, and still a few others were thespians or science whiz kids. Sadly, many of them tried to live "today" as a reprise of their high school days. It rarely works. Past glories often dim present possibilities, and many teenage stars never achieve as adults what they could have because today never has the luster of yesterday.

Past glories can steal our joy. They must be let go. Yesterday's popularity all too easily limits today's possibilities. We can be proud of past achievements. There's nothing wrong with that. All too often, however, when today's opportunities are seen in the light of yesterday's remembered glories, they can never measure up and so today becomes one disappointment after another.

In the Old Testament God calls Israel to let past glories go so they can see what God is creating in the present for their future:

> Thus says the Lord, who makes a way in the sea, a path in the mighty waters, who brings out chariot and horse, army and warrior; they lie down, they cannot rise, they are extinguished, quenched like a wick. Do not remember the former, or consider the things of old. I am about to do a new thing; now it springs forth, do you not perceive it? I will make a way in the wilderness and rivers in the desert. The wild animals will honor me, the jackals and the ostriches; for I give water in the wilderness, rivers in the desert, to give drink to my chosen people, the people whom I formed for myself so that they might declare my praise. (Isaiah 43:16-21)

God is doing "a new thing." But unless the people of God are willing to unlearn yesterday's miracles—the great event of the Exodus—they simply will not be able to see what God is doing today that is different from the past. "Do not remember the former, or consider the things of old. I am about to do a new thing; now it springs forth, do you not perceive it" (18-19b)?

We are not called to forget the evil of the past. Rather, God is telling us that unless we are willing to set aside the glories of the past we will not be able to discover the presence of the God of joy in our today.

TAKING LEAVE OF TOMORROW

There is still another leave taking we must choose if we are to know joy. We fully live today by taking leave of tomorrow as well.

All too many people lose the potential for joy in their lives by worrying about tomorrow. They seem to live today as if tomorrow will bring nothing but the worst to them. These people are more than pessimistic; they squander their today on the possibility that tomorrow will undo the present moment's hope and promise. Rather than simply enjoy the day and all its potential, they worry. They seem to think that enjoying today will inevitably set themselves up for problems tomorrow.

> By living each day fully in trust and joy we will discover that God does not disappear when bad things happen to us, and neither does joy.

Jesus knew about our penchant for worrying and he advised against it:

> Therefore I tell you, do not worry about your life, what you will eat or what you will drink, or about your body, what you will wear. Is not life more than food, and the body more than clothing? Look at the birds of the air, they neither sow nor reap nor gather in to barns, and yet your heavenly Father feeds them. Are you not of more value than they? And can any of you by worrying add a single hour to your span of life?" (Matthew 6:25-27)

The antidote to worry is trust. Trust adds depth to our days. Worry creates an energy drain that exacts a cost on today—and on tomorrow when it becomes today. Yet our worst fears rarely come true. Our deepest anxieties almost never come to pass. Why then, should we allow worry to compromise the joy of this day? It is far better to trust that God is with us in *this* day and then eagerly look for signs of his gracious and loving presence.

If it should happen that our worst fears do come to pass, worrying beforehand will rarely prepare us for it. By living each day fully in trust and joy we will discover that God does not disappear when bad things happen to us, and neither does joy.

The wisdom of Jesus is that today is enough to pay attention to. If we are willing to live fully in this day, setting aside our anxieties and fears for tomorrow, our hearts will be open to the many gifts that God brings to us in each present moment, and we will know joy. God knows what we need and will encourage us to make reasonable provisions for tomorrow.

A few years ago I was driving across the great state of Montana. It is indeed Big Sky Country and it takes many hours to traverse its boundaries. We were listening to the radio as we traveled through the beauty of Montana, but the further we got from the city where the station broadcast its signal, the worse the signal became. We began to notice that we were driving out of the station's range by the initial, light static we heard. In a few minutes, however, the static grew to such an extent that the signal was lost. We no longer heard any music. We just heard noise.

Worry is spiritual static that drowns out the music of God's grace. The signal—the promises of God in Jesus Christ—is lost in the overwhelming noise of our fears. We can only embrace the possibility of joy in our lives today by learning to take leave of our worries about tomorrow.

SEEING TODAY AS MORE THAN A PRELUDE TO TOMORROW

But worry is not the only thing that prevents us from living joyfully in the here and now. Losing today by living in tomorrow also happens when today is seen as a mere prelude to tomorrow. Tomorrow is our hope and promise. Today is only to be endured in order to get to tomorrow.

"I wished we hadn't waited," my father said. He had just purchased a recreational vehicle and it was a beauty. The length was 32 feet, it had a queen size bed and a kitchenette, television and bathroom all enclosed. This was the dream that my father and mother had shared. When he retired, they would buy their R.V. and travel together.

But my mother died suddenly at the age of fifty-nine, the night before her sixtieth birthday. Dad worked for four more years and then, upon retiring, he purchased their dream recreational vehicle. It was a bittersweet moment because the life partner with whom he had shared the dream was gone.

They had enough money when mom was still alive, but they wanted to save up a bit more, wait until retirement, and then put the money to work realizing their dream. Dad sadly acknowledged to me that he had lost so many "todays" with mom by living in the "tomorrow" that never came.

> We let joy slip through our grasp when we live today as if tomorrow is when joy will certainly come.

We let joy slip through our grasp when we live today as if tomorrow is when joy will certainly come. Tomorrow we will have what we most want. Tomorrow we will have the time and the resources to do what we most desire today— tomorrow . . . and tomorrow . . . and tomorrow.

But tomorrow is not real. Of course we should plan for tomorrow. But if we postpone truly living today for the sake of tomorrow, we bet our lives on long odds. The days of joy that my parents dreamed of never occurred. And in the process they lost a possibility that was truly present to them.

I have been a pastor for over thirty years. In all that time I have had the privilege of being at the bedside of countless men and women who were dying or near death. Some had been highly successful professionals. Others were laborers who had worked hard all their lives to achieve some degree of financial security. In all of those moments, I have never heard anyone say that they wished they could have spent more time in the office or on plans for tomorrow. Yet, countless times I have heard them lament over missed opportunities for joy with friends and family lost because they were living today as if it was no more than a prelude to tomorrow.

Jesus invites us to joy. He asks us to trust that tomorrow will bring both challenges and the ability to meet the challenges when it comes. The Savior invites us to live in today by responsibly planning for tomorrow and then trusting the God of tomorrow to meet us there. Don't lose the joy of today by using it for the tomorrow that may never come.

QUESTIONS FOR FURTHER REFLECTION

❧ In the light of your faith, how would you describe the significance of your life today?

❧ How has the significance of your life changed over the years as your life circumstances have changed?

❧ How might prayer add to the significance of your life?

❧ What might you need to leave behind to have a more purposeful, significant life?

❦ How might forgiveness help you to live purposefully and significantly today?

❦ What old assumptions do you need to be free from in order to live well in this changing world?

❦ What would it mean for you to "take leave of tomorrow?"

CHAPTER THREE

Unleashing Your Passion

It is having a purpose that goes beyond yourself that makes life joyful and worth living. According to Arthur C. Hall:

> God has a purpose for each one of us, a work for each one to do, a place for each one to fill, an influence for each one to exert, a likeness to his dear Son for each one to manifest, and then, a place for each one to fill in his holy temple. (Wallace, 1983)

Passion and purpose go hand in hand. Passion is the emotional component of purpose. Without passion, purpose is just an idea. When passion is combined with an opportunity, purpose is born. Purpose is passion with focus. Purpose is the aim in life that directs passion toward a goal that is beyond the immediate. But what is purpose? How do we discover it in our own lives?

Disciples of Jesus understand purpose as a spiritual blessing. If spirituality is that which brings together all the disparate parts of our lives under the reign of God, then purpose is the spiritual force that shapes our lives.

The problem is that many of us misunderstand purpose. We think of purpose as a one-time revelation. We believe that our purpose in life is a once and for all discovery of the direction our life should take.

Instead, purpose, as the focus of our passion, is an ever evolving sense of who we are and what we can (and must) accomplish. Purpose is the unleashing of our passion in life.

Purpose changes as we change. The focus (purpose) of our lives will shift as our circumstances, awareness, and relationships change. The truth of the matter is that our life purpose is rarely set openly before us. It emerges, instead, out of the chance encounters and daily discoveries of life.

An individual attends a concert and the symphony is more than the sum total of the instruments in the orchestra. The symphony emerges as the music and the life of the listener converge in a poetry of sound and breath. From that experience, a composer is born. Or, from that experience, a conductor is forged in the imagination and joy of a child.

On a more ordinary level, a child attends worship at a local church. As the pastor intones the liturgy or preaches God's Word, the child's imagination is set afire and life and truth come together in his or her heart. Suddenly a girl or boy begins to dream of sharing such life transforming words with others and a pastor is born. The work God has for each of us to do is born from the passions that spring from the depth of our hearts and minds as we engage life.

There is no particular situation, no set plan that unleashes the passion of a person. The most important influence that you and I may have in the life of our families, friends, and colleagues will not come from one stellar moment—but rather from the accumulation of a life well lived before them.

I remember as a child my grandfather standing in front of a field of forty acres. We had driven by this same field the night before. Then the soy beans stood strong and tall, green leaves waving in the breeze, the promise of a harvest rich and plentiful. Now we stood before the same field after a devastating storm. It looked like elephants had trampled and rolled over the green leaves leaving a sodden acreage of broken stems and shredded plants.

I stood in mute awe before this terrible destruction. Finally, I turned to my grandfather and asked, "Grandpa, what will you do?"

Without turning to look at me, my grandfather simply replied, "God will give us another year, Mike. God will give us another year."

This episode remains in my imagination because over the years I shared with my grandfather, I came to understand that his faith was a living thing that empowered him to survive—no, thrive!—through unimaginably difficult experiences such as the loss of three farms and the deaths of two beloved children. My grandfather didn't hold onto his faith. His faith held onto him. When everything else seemed vacuous, his faith in the Savior who promised an abundant life sustained him. His life became a witness of purpose and passion that I couldn't understand until I had grown to adulthood and lived through my own pain and disappointments.

> Purpose is passion with the focus of *this* day and *these* relationships in the possibilities of God's love.

So often we pass right by the purpose our God is calling us to because we look for a single moment, a particular revelation that will clarify why we are here and what we are to do. God doesn't work that way. The disciple of Jesus understands that our God comes to us in the changing relationships and circumstances of our lives. Passion is rarely unleashed in a moment of blinding clarity. Passion comes into focus over time. As our passions begin to find their focus, our purpose emerges.

As my grandfather was able to look beyond what seemed an "obvious" tragedy to the shaping and sustaining grace of God, we too must learn to look beyond and live beyond the "obvious" meaning of our lives if we are to discover real purpose and real passion. The great treasures of life are hidden beneath the "obvious," beneath the surface meanings we find as we think about this day, this relationship, and the events in which we find ourselves.

There is no more a magic formula for finding purpose than there is a magic potion for solving the problems of life. The Holy Spirit touches real people in the real relationships and circumstances of their lives and opens them to the best of who they are and what they can do. Purpose is passion with the focus of *this* day and *these* relationships in the possibilities of God's love.

FINDING PURPOSE IN LIVING BEYOND OURSELVES

The work to which our God calls us is not a singular, life transforming labor. Instead it evolves. To know joy from day to day we must always live with passion focused by purpose, but our passions and purposes will change as we move through life. One thing they will always have in common, however, is that true passion and purpose will always take us beyond ourselves.

Many of us are misled into believing that our life purposes are confirmed by the recognition of others. It rarely works that way. Few of us can recall the life of Howard Hughes, a man who lived at the epicenter of his generation. He hobnobbed with the rich and famous. He was on a first name basis with presidents and starlets. His designs for aircraft were considered remarkable and on the leading edge of technology. He was rewarded by fame and fortune becoming one of the most wealthy of men of his time. Yet today he is almost forgotten.

On the other hand, a young nun, following the calling of God, was willing to launch out in ministry without the blessing of her bishop. Renouncing the position and privilege of teaching at a prestigious girls' school, she entered the streets of Calcutta to embrace the poorest of the poor in the name of Jesus Christ. Out of her focused passion for society's disposable people, God raised her up and she traveled the globe. She became an emissary to presidents and prime ministers. Few of us can picture the visage of Howard Hughes, but most of us can conjure up a picture of a simple nun who came to be known as Mother Teresa of Calcutta, the woman who reminded us that although we may not all do "great" things, we can (and must) do all things with great love.

The difference? One lived for this world and the immediate gratification of wealth and fame. The other spent her life for eternal purposes. One is relegated to the footnotes of American history. The other stands as a timeless witness to what one person can accomplish when passion is unleashed with focus for a purpose beyond the self.

Dr. Mark Zipper of Allina Health Systems has said that positive psychology has identified three elements essential for a life of joy. The first element is work that matters. The second is relationships that work. The third is a purpose beyond the self.

What is fascinating is that a purpose beyond oneself is necessary in order for the other two essentials (work and relationships) to be developed. No one can have work that matters if it only provides a paycheck. Work that matters contributes to the well-being of others. I remember a friend in Salem, What a remarkable concept: we live beyond ourselves through those we love.

Oregon who was a garbage collector. When I asked him about his work he smiled and said, "I don't collect garbage. I prevent pestilence and disease." What I discovered was a highly educated man who connected his labor with the health of the community in which he and his family lived.

How can relationships matter if they have no purpose beyond themselves? My father taught me that marriage is not simply a relationship between a man and a woman, as wonderful as that can be. It was the gift of family. More than that, it was the source of identity for me and my brothers.

I remember once when I was going out on an important date my father looked up from his newspaper and, after learning of my evening plans, simply said, "Mike, remember: you're a Foss." It was his way of saying that my relationship with my girlfriend was not separate from who I was as his son. I came to understand that my father and mother saw their love extending outward through the lives of their sons.

What a remarkable concept: we live beyond ourselves through those we love and the labor we give is not just to make a living but to help create a world worthy of those we most love! Relationships matter when we see them as the fertile soil from which a healthy tomorrow can grow.

When we look at our work and our relationships in the context of our own mortality, it becomes clear that only a purpose beyond ourselves can add meaning and joy.

OUR PURPOSES AND GOD'S PURPOSES

I do not know when I will die. I know that I will, but the when and how and why of it is not in my ability to foresee. Disciples understand, however, that our dying will not be the consequence of a random lottery or mere chance. I do not mean to say that God causes our deaths. Rather, I want to assert that none of us dies without the love and purpose of God being present. The purpose of your life is contained within God's purposes.

This is not to dismiss all the questions that arise from the tragic and premature deaths of others. I simply acknowledge that I do not understand why some die far too early while others seemingly live far too long. Here we run into the limits of human understanding. I am willing, however, to trust that our God will not be absent nor inattentive at the moment of my death or your death. This loving attention from our Creator God places our lives within a larger purpose that can serve forever.

The alignment of our personal purposes as they emerge and evolve over time with the purposes of God happens when we begin to reflect in our lives the character of Christ. Our Lord's character is not revealed in us through moral perfection. Rather, the character of Christ is disclosed when we dare to hope in a hopeless time. When we can see the possibilities of the kingdom of God in the midst of pain and suffering, we disclose the character of Christ.

When we dare to love in a selfish world, Christ is revealed in our lives. When, instead of living for what we can get in possessions, power, and privilege, we live for the sake of others, we disclose Christ—and we inspire others to also live beyond themselves in love.

> Live in the confidence that "the one who is in you is greater than the one who is in the world" (1 John 4:4b).

That's the difference between a Howard Hughes and a Mother Teresa (or any other true follower of Christ).

Was such a purpose filled and joyful life possible for Howard Hughes? Yes, of course. Unfortunately he couldn't (or wouldn't) imagine it and so he couldn't live into it.

The character of Jesus is further disclosed when we live courageously in a world dominated by fear and anxiety. I am struck by the free-floating anxiety of our time. People are worried, and often they don't know what they are worried about. Whether it is the war in Iraq, dwindling oil reserves, fear over our economy, fear of international terrorism, or the terrorism of street gangs in our cities, we live in a time characterized by fear of the known and unknown. Christians, however, live in the confidence that "the one who is in you is greater than the one who is in the world" (1 John 4:4b). That one who is in us is Christ, and the very character of Christ is revealed in us when we refuse to give in to the anxiety of our times.

Jesus, standing before Pilate, declared that only God gives authority in any ultimate sense. Whether he lived or died, our Lord clearly lived in the confidence that our Creator God was still in charge. This placed his particular situation in the larger context of God's eternal will. Disciples understand that our circumstances are circumscribed by the grace of God. We are not afraid. Our purpose is sealed in the divine purposes of eternity.

Are you worried about tomorrow? Look to Jesus who could trust God in the face of his own inevitable death, and know that the Spirit of Jesus is within you, transforming you to Christ-likeness (2 Corinthians 3:17-18).

Do you imagine all sorts of potentially ruinous outcomes of this or that action? Place your fears in the hands of the God who desires only good for you and creation. Trust God with your actions, assuming (of course) that you have taken the time to plan well and focus your passion. Act in the faith that: "It is God who is at work in you, enabling you both to will and to work for his good pleasure" (Philippians 2:13).

THE DESTINY OF DISCIPLES

Are you stuck in life? Do you believe your circumstances are so immoveable and unchangeable that you can no longer hope in the Risen One? Look to Christ whose hope conquered death itself and now, on the other side of death, "intercedes for us" (Romans 8:34) as we live this life in faith and love.

The call of discipleship is a call to an unending life of purpose and joy—a forever destiny. The book of Ephesians gives voice to this destiny:

> Blessed be the God and Father of our Lord Jesus Christ, who has blessed us in Christ with every spiritual blessing in the heavenly places, just as he chose us in Christ before the foundation of the world to be holy and blameless before him in love. . . . For by grace you have been saved through faith, and this is not your own doing; it is the gift of God—not the result of works, so that no one may boast. For we are what he has made us, created in Christ Jesus for good works, which God prepared beforehand to be our way of life. (Ephesians 1:3-4; 2:8-10)

The blessing of the disciple is the plan of God. The good pleasure of God's will is that we might experience passion with a focus and live with the joy of purpose. This joy of purpose is the purpose of God (love) alive within and through us in our world.

Christians believe that God, in the wisdom of eternity, has chosen to partner with human beings to make this world fit for the kingdom of the Son, Jesus Christ. We do not presume to believe that God *needs us*. Instead, out of the love that created all that is, God has chosen to work within and through us.

This is a great mystery! Why God should choose to be at work primarily through Christ's universal Church is beyond our imagining. After all, our God is capable of accomplishing anything and everything that God purposes.

That notwithstanding, God has chosen us to be vehicles for eternal good. And what is required is our willingness to be what God has chosen us to be, to do what God has chosen us to do.

Our willingness to follow Jesus in the way of God becomes the doorway through which the grace, love, mercy, and justice of God enter our world. It is Christ at work within and through us that makes this divine-human partnership possible.

So purpose is more than mere wishful thinking! Purpose is the point of contact between my life and the will of God. Purpose cannot be measured, therefore, by the standards of worldly success. By the standards of worldly success Jesus was clearly a Our "faith working through love" (Galatians 5:6) graces the lives of those around us in ways only God can fully know. failure—a peasant teacher executed for sedition. By God's standards, however, Jesus' passion and faithfulness led not to failure but to both victory over death and to the establishment of a community of faith where God's love is the foundation stone.

God's purposes are measured in the blessings—both visible and invisible—that our lives of passion and faithfulness bring to the lives of others. Herein is our destiny. Our "faith working through love" (Galatians 5:6) graces the lives of those around us in ways only God can fully know. Our confidence is in the promise that such grace is surely at work within and through us.

AN ETERNAL LEGACY OF FAITH
God has also given us who live out our faith an eternal legacy. The love we leave in the lives of others will outlast our own lives and resound in glory to God.

I remember being in worship with my mother and father. Looking up, I noticed my dad didn't close his eyes during the prayers. Later I asked my father if he didn't believe. After all, my child's mind concluded, if you believe, you close your eyes in prayer. My father simply replied that God could hear him whether he had his eyes closed or opened. My father's faith was not a formula, not a rite or a ritual, not a duty or an obligation. His faith was a relationship of trust and love with the God who made him and accepted him for who he was.

Over the years I have come to understand that God desires a real relationship with real people—real living and breathing people who are in the thick of life and who pray with their eyes closed or open.

As I shared in chapter one of this book, God does not ask us to be what and who we cannot be. God is not looking for plaster saints. God is looking for honest relationships with real flesh and blood people— warts and all, fallibilities and all, sins, weaknesses and all. The transforming power of God's Spirit can take us as we are and mold our passions to God's purposes, and in the doing of it give us joy like we have never known—if we are willing.

> God's will (love) is the purpose beyond ourselves that is worthy of our living into. Anything less than this is simply unworthy of our lives.

The purposes of God work most powerfully within and through us when we are real. To paraphrase an old rabbinic story, after we have left this life we should not fear that God will ask: "Why were you not more like St. Francis or Mother Teresa or Martin Luther King, Jr.?" Rather, we should fear that he will ask us, "Why were you not more like yourself? Why did you not become all that I created you to be?" "Where is *your* legacy?"

Through the real events of our own lives, through the give and take of our own many relationships, through the ups and downs of our own achievements and failures, as we develop our own unique gifts and abilities and mold our own passion to God's purposes, God will draw out from who we are a life that points to who God is.

In the Lord's Prayer we pray: "Thy will be done on earth as it is in heaven." Luther reminds us that we do not pray for the will of God to be accomplished. After all, it shall be as God wishes! Instead we pray that God's will shall be done in and through us. God's will (love) is the purpose beyond ourselves that is worthy of our living into. Anything less than this is simply unworthy of our lives.

GRASPING OPPORTUNITIES THROUGH FAITH

The question still remains, however: How can we set our passions free to serve God's purposes? In a word, passion is unleashed through opportunity grasped.

Dr. Fenwick Huss had just finished his class on accounting when an international student from China approached him. "Dr. Huss, my country needs what you are teaching. Would you consider going to China to teach?"

Dr. Huss, thinking it would never happen, said, "Yes."

To his great surprise, a few weeks later opportunity came knocking. Dr. Huss received a letter from the Chinese Ministry of Aviation requesting him to come to China and teach. Could he arrive on a given day and at a given time at the airport in Guangzhou? Travel arrangements would be made for him by the government of China.

Dr. Huss grasped the opportunity. It matched his abilities and his passions. He did the previously unimaginable: he made the trip to China and was given high marks from the Chinese government for the excellence and effectiveness of his teaching.

The result of that simple exchange between a student and a professor was an unlocking of opportunity that, with its subsequent accomplishment, has continued to fan the flames of passion. Now serving as Dean of Robinson College of Business at Georgia State University, Dr. Huss has traveled extensively throughout Europe, Russia, and Asia. His goal: to equip people of any nation to succeed in world business. As a reflection of his faith and his commitment to the purposes of God, there is a Habitat for Humanity house in Siberia that Dr. Huss's work funded.

The steps to unleashing our passions are simple and consecutive. The first step is coming to a faith-centered openness to what God is able to do in the opportunities we grasp. When our hearts and minds are open to the possibility that God will open us to more of ourselves if we grasp the opportunities before us that answer to our passions and abilities, we will be more likely to respond. For Fenwick Huss, his love of teaching, his interest in business, his love of travel, and his compassion for people around the world combined to spread the fruit of his passion and purpose.

The second step to unleashing our passion is acting on our openness. Many opportunities are lost to us because between the asking and the doing life gets in the way. We succumb to the "tyranny of the urgent" rather than live in the freedom of the possible. Our fear of the unknown, our addiction to control, and our unwillingness to move out of our comfort zones can block us from acting on the invitation to purpose. These and other internal safe guards can work to protect us from unnecessary difficulty or danger, to be sure, but they can also prevent us from walking through a door that God has purposefully opened before us.

The third step is to reflect on our experience and decide if, having grasped an opportunity, we accomplished what we had intended. More importantly we ask ourselves if the experience gave us a sense of energy and inner joy. If the answer to both questions is positive, it is likely that God has indeed invited us to unleash our passions for a purpose that is worth our lives.

When Susan Cordell was invited by her pastor to join the staff of her local congregation, she was dumbfounded. She had a successful career that she loved in the hospitality industry. But, try as she would, she couldn't dismiss the invitation and the opportunity. It kept coming back to her, teasing her mind, making her wonder just what God might be doing.

With the support of her husband, Susan left her career for what she thought would be a short-term opportunity to help her church grow. Now, nearly twenty years later, it is obvious to those who know her that God matched her inner passion with a new purpose. The combination of her executive skills in the hospitality industry and her deep faith in Jesus Christ empowered the ministry team whose work has led to a thriving church in Midtown Atlanta.

Joy is the result of passions unleashed for purposeful living. Joy deepens over time, not in a single instant. Joy is the outcome of our ongoing connection to God, the best of ourselves, and the world around us.

Joy is a disciple's birthright. Discipleship is not an intellectual exercise; it is a way of living that is centered in daily practices that open us to see the power of God already present and active in our lives. In the next chapter we will explore these practices in order to lay a foundation for a life of joy.

QUESTIONS FOR FURTHER REFLECTION

❦ What are your particular passions right now?

❦ If they are not already, how might you begin focusing your passions so they serve a purpose beyond yourself?

❦ What does it mean to say that our relationships need a purpose beyond themselves to be truly healthy?

❦ What blessings do your passions, purpose, and faithfulness bring to the lives of others?

❦ Do you feel like you are becoming all that God created you to be? If not, why not?

❦ Are there any new or surprising opportunities in front of you right now to unleash your passions for a purpose beyond yourself?

CHAPTER FOUR

Growing into Eternity

Helen Keller once wrote, "I believe in the immortality of the soul because I have within me immortal longings" (Wallace, 1983). Joy is the soul's response when our immortal longings touch their source and end—the Triune God. Just as our God has placed within us such deep longings, so does God continue to awaken them in us so that they might grow us into forever.

Eternity is often thought of as a time that exists independent of this life with its limitations of time and space. The idea of forever as that time into which we emerge upon death is, however, a denial of eternity. *The invitation to practice the Marks of Discipleship is an invitation to see more fully and claim more strongly the work of God.* Eternity, by definition, is not limited by time— past, present, future—but is the source of our time. As such, forever is co-existent with our time. Eternity is now, or as Paul said: "Now is the day of salvation" (2 Corinthians 6:2). This life is a wonderful opportunity to live within the abundance of forever by growing into eternity.

The Father has created us for eternity. The Son, Jesus, invites us to see eternity in his resurrection and claim it as the promise of our faith. The Holy Spirit works to activate our immortal longings and awaken us to the presence of forever in our daily lives. In the grand scheme of things, this is how God develops a real faith within us for our real lives. The events, choices, relationships, and circumstances of our lives serve as the raw materials of God's faith-building work. Which is to say that there is great significance in our daily lives, in what we do and how we do it under the leading of God's Spirit.

The invitation to practice the *Marks of Discipleship* is an invitation to see more fully and claim more strongly the work of God. As our faith (trust) finds its center in Jesus Christ and as the Holy Spirit dissolves the separation between faith and life, faithfulness in living each moment in sync with the purposes of God becomes possible.

She had called from the hospital. She was with her mother in another city and was facing the most difficult decision she had ever dealt with: the doctors were asking her to decide whether to put a feeding tube in and prolong her mother's life or not.

We talked for a long time. She shared how her mother had always told her to let her go when the time came, but there had been no living will. Now, she had to decide. We prayed. We talked about our confidence in life after death and our belief that death is the final healer. Then we prayed again. The next I heard from her was when her mother passed away two days later. It had happened much more quickly than anyone had anticipated.

Now, she and her husband and I were sharing breakfast as I spoke of grief and loss. "You know," I gently said, "many people experience the presence of the deceased in a wonderful way. If this happens to you, don't think you're crazy. It just happens. And don't be afraid."

They looked at each other and then she shared how they had been sleeping in her mother's bedroom two days after the funeral. They had been working to clean things up, setting some things aside for a garage sale and setting other things aside to keep or give away. They were exhausted. Suddenly, in the middle of the night, they both awakened simultaneously and sat bolt upright in bed. Looking at the squeaking rocking chair, they saw her mother. She was sitting there and simply smiled at them. Then she disappeared.

With tears streaming down her eyes, she said, "I would have thought I was crazy but we both saw the same thing at the same time. And I know she came back to tell me it was okay—I had made the right decision for her."

For over thirty years of ministry and through nearly seven years of serving in hospice, I have heard many stories like the one above. At first I responded with scientific-religious skepticism: the events described were projections of inner turmoil or illusions of misplaced hope. But the more I listened and tested what I heard, the more open I became. There were, to be sure, some stories that did not ring true. But the majority of stories, shared only after careful listening and permission giving, as with the couple above, had the ring of truth to them.

These stories not only rang true but shared many elements. There was no disassociation from reality. The people knew where they were, who they were, and the circumstances of their lives. The stories often reflected the astonishment of those who experienced them, as well as a sense of the sacred, and an unwillingness to share the event for fear of ridicule or being dismissed. The more I listened the more I discovered that a wide variety of people, from all walks of life and levels of education, have experienced a seeing beyond the obvious.

This judgment has been confirmed in a study by Brayne and others of the Palliative Care Team at Camden Primary Care Trust, London, England (2006). Their study concluded that deathbed phenomenon (DBP) are regularly reported as an important part of the dying process. They also concluded that DBP are far broader than the traditional image of an apparition at the end of the bed, are most likely not drug induced, and that patients were more likely to talk with nurses rather than doctors about their experience. The point is that such phenomena are much more real and evident in human experience than we had traditionally thought. More than that, they are not the result of drugs or projections as traditionally understood.

My interest was piqued when I noted that those who had these experiences reported a deepening of faith and confidence, a stronger sense of well-being in the face of upsetting changes, and an astonishing lack of fear of death. Their lives had been blessed with joy.

PRACTICING OUR FAITH

Recently, I began to explore studies done on the effects of religious practice on longevity and health. Most medical and psychological studies now begin with the assumption that an active religious life positively affects one's well-being. The question of how that happens—and how the medical or psychological practitioner can help facilitate it in the life of the patient—is most frequently the focus of attention.

For example, a recent study (Consedine, et. al., 2004) conducted at Long Island University in New York of 1,118 adults aged 65-86 years of age measured the trait "joy" and the trait "interest" following differential emotions theory. What they found was remarkable. The trait "interest," associated with higher education (interest being simply defined as intellectual engagement in life), showed no positive impact on morbidity (length of life) and was associated with greater stress than the norm. On the other

The benefits of faith (joy!) are most readily present in the lives of those who engage in living their beliefs through the practices of religion.

hand, the trait "joy" (happiness) was associated with greater religious participation and resulted in lower morbidity and stress than the norm.

It is important to note that joy is associated with *greater religious participation*. We have discovered that meaningful religion is not merely intellectual. Effective belief is also behavioral. The benefits of faith (joy!) are most readily present in the lives of those who engage in living their beliefs through the practices of religion.

THE MARKS OF DISCIPLESHIP

That's what the *Marks of Discipleship* are all about. They are not ends in themselves. Instead, by practicing them we develop lives that reflect our "immortal longings" and open us to eternity daily. It is not surprising that increased quality and length of life are consistently observed in those who practice their faith. I suggest this ought not be surprising simply because the more frequently we approach the God of life, the more life, in all of its aspects, will be present in us.

When life is more fully lived, we not only deepen our inner selves but we engage more deeply with others. The disciplines or practices of the Christian life are designed to help us live life more fully.

The *Marks of Discipleship* are divided into two particular sections. The first three—*Daily Prayer*, *Weekly Worship*, and *Daily Bible Reading*—focus on the practice of personal disciplines that grow us deeper in faith. The second three—*Serve Within and Beyond the Congregation*, *Relate to Others for Spiritual Growth*, and *Give a Tithe and Beyond*—call us outward in service to the world God loves.

We simply cannot grow in our relationship with God if (1) we do not tend to that relationship, and (2) we do not allow God to send us out into the world. This inward-outward movement of faith continues throughout our lives.

The *Marks of Discipleship* are not a check list for the super spiritual nor are they ways of controlling God—as if that were possible. They are biblical and historic spiritual disciplines that grow eternity within the human soul. The point of the practices is to develop a more confident and joyful relationship with God in Jesus Christ in which our lives are good for ourselves and good for others.

Daily Prayer. Daily prayer is not a method for gaining power over God. Instead, true prayer invites us into a dynamic relationship with the God who alone is God. That relationship is typified by trust in God, not power over God. We pray recognizing our limitations and trusting the One who is above such limitations.

The recent spate of studies on the affects of prayer on those recovering from surgery or those facing significant medical issues has left us with confusing results. On the one hand, we have studies that conclude that prayer positively affects the recovery rate and lessens the possibility of relapse. On the other hand, we have recent studies that reach the opposite conclusions! How can disciples of Jesus who believe in the power of prayer make sense out of this?

I suggest that this confusion of outcomes is understandable because we are measuring the wrong thing. If prayer gave us power to control both life and God, then studying the outcomes of prayer would make sense. But, as prayer cannot deliver on either, the power of prayer can only be measured in the benefits it brings through a deeper relationship with Jesus Christ. What are the benefits of prayer rightly understood?

First, I would suggest that prayer is God's gift of vision. Daily prayer creates within us the vision to see God at work in our world as well as the ability to trust that God is at work in the world when we cannot see it clearly.

We had gathered in the hospital room for the final vigil. Jean was dying. The cancer that had been beaten back by chemo-therapy had surged forward and over-whelmed her body. She had suffered much, and now, as the hour of her death drew near, I gathered with her family for prayer.

> Prayer opens our hearts to see from a different vantage point.

Her husband held her hand and silently prayed. Then, looking up with tears in his eyes, he asked, "Why hasn't God taken her, Pastor Mike? Why doesn't God take her?" Then he fled the room.

Two of his children left to care for their grief-stricken father. I took his place and soothed her fevered brow with the cool water beside her bed, gently wiping her forehead with a damp washcloth. What was God up to? I wondered. Why were these wonderful people going through all of this for so long? Then it happened.

During all the hours we had gathered, one son had sat as far from his mother as physically possible in that hospital room. He had found the furthest corner and stayed safely there. Now, his father having fled, this young man got up from the floor and approached his mother's death bed. He asked me to step aside, took the washcloth from my hands, and wiped his mother's feverish brow. Then he leaned down and gently said, "I love you mom. It's okay for you to go now. It's okay mom." And his mother took a breath and entered into forever.

That was when I realized that relational healing had taken place. We had prayed for a miracle of healing—and it had happened. It just wasn't what we had thought it would be.

Prayer opens our hearts to see from a different vantage point. Prayer makes it possible for us to see miracles that may come in ways other than what we had anticipated and prayed for. Only prayer, daily prayer, can open us to see how the The discipline of daily prayer gives us a new perspective on the ordinary realities of life.

Spirit moves in our lives and in our world. Without a life of daily prayer, I don't believe I would have seen what God had done that afternoon. Prayer, by opening us to the possibility of forever, places the particular moments of our lives in the context of eternity.

Hence the need for *daily* prayer. The content of our lives is made up of today's activities, today's relationships, today's opportunities and challenges, as well as today's hopes and fears. There is, however, a deeper, spiritual dimension to our lives that we become aware of through prayer. Which is to say that the discipline of daily prayer gives us a new perspective on the ordinary realities of life.

Without daily prayer we can't get beyond the physical and psychological/emotional aspects of life. We cling, therefore, to the physical life of a loved one in the hope that our emotional connection with them will be prolonged.

Prayer, however, sets the physical life of the one we love in the context of a spiritual and eternal life, and the promise of living relationships that will not end. Only from that perspective could the miracle of healing between that son and his mother be made visible. Her death was a simple but profound affirmation of God's act of healing. And her death was not her end. Her son knew that and so was able to reconcile and let her go.

Prayer also opens our hearts to the blessing of serenity. Serenity is an inner calm born of spiritual confidence. Serenity is *shalom*—a Hebrew word that means complete well-being. In the face of challenge, difficulty, or suffering, serenity is that equanimity of spirit that trusts the presence of God.

Serenity arises from trust—trust in the providence of God that empowers us to discern what we can influence and what is beyond our influence. Daily prayer is a discipline that plants serenity in our lives. The benefits of serenity are both the ability to let go and let God deal with those things that are out of our control or influence and the ability to act on what we know we can deal with.

The power to let go of what is beyond us is, in fact, necessary if we are going to be effective in areas where we do have some control or influence. Only when we are no longer distracted by what we cannot do can we focus and act on what we can do. The experience of serenity in the face of life's challenges and opportunities is an amazing gift to those who come to God in prayer on a daily basis.

The serenity we experience from disciplined daily prayer is closely related to another great benefit of regular prayer: inner strength in times of powerlessness.

"There's nothing I can do," she sighed. "I feel so helpless—and I'm not used to feeling helpless."

She and her husband had been struggling to have a family for several years. They had spent thousands of dollars on tests, treatments, and medical initiatives to overcome her infertility. Now, the latest attempt had proven ineffective. An executive in a national advertising firm, she was used to being in charge and getting things done. But now she was facing a situation that she couldn't change.

"Where is God in all this, anyway? Why am I being punished when I see people who have children and don't even know how to care for them?" she exclaimed.

"There is one power you have left," I said. "I know it sounds a bit naive, but we can pray. I'd like to pray for your healing, and I'd like to pray for inner strength, and for the vision to see what you can do. Prayer can help you to feel some inner power now that you recognize that you are powerless to change your situation."

She was understandably dubious, but we prayed together and she agreed to pray daily until we met again in two weeks.

Two weeks later she shared that she was still frustrated. "But," she said, "somehow I feel better when I pray. I tell God everything he already knows— how angry and sad I am. But I also

> Inner strength, like serenity, only grows (and flourishes) in the harsh climate of adversity.

tell him that I'm open to whatever he gives. It's helping. When I pray I actually feel like I'm doing something not just waiting for some medical miracle."

Prayer should not be the last thing we do. Prayer should be the first thing we do. The prayer of faith can create within us a hope that opens the future again. The disciple of Jesus knows that prayer is active; we are doing something in prayer, the results of which we may not be able to predict or foresee at the moment, but something *always* happens when we pray.

From this sense of power in our powerlessness comes an inner strength that flourishes in our weakness. In her weakness, the woman who wanted to be a mother discovered an inner reserve that she had not needed before. When dealing with previous difficulties she always had the tools needed to meet the challenge. But she couldn't change her own biology. When medical science proved unable to heal her, daily prayer grew an inner strength enabling her to face with serenity whatever her future brought.

I am not suggesting that prayer cannot or does not heal. On the contrary, it has been my privilege to experience healing prayer that resulted in supra-medical healing. Prayer may indeed heal the medical condition that makes pregnancy impossible for my friend. If that is the only result that we will accept as an answer to prayer, however, we have limited the unlimited; we have circumscribed God's wisdom and activity by our lack of vision and faith.

Inner strength cannot grow from always having things our own way. Inner strength, like serenity, only grows (and flourishes) in the harsh climate of adversity.

Besides, all physical healing is temporary. Only the spiritual healing of faith itself is eternal. Those who were healed by the Savior during his earthly ministry later became ill and died. Even Lazarus, though raised from the dead, eventually died.

How can we practice daily prayer? Begin at a level that makes sense in your present situation. If you are going to begin daily prayer for the first time, find a simple devotional book. Read it and then repeat the prayer that is often included. As time goes on, you'll find that you'll want to add to that prayer. Let the Holy Spirit lead you into this next stage of prayer development.

Next, make a prayer list of the persons or situations you want to talk to God about. Go through the list each day in prayer. Keep track of changes in the circumstances of those for whom you pray or resolutions to the situations for which you pray. Write these alongside your list and watch how the Holy Spirit deepens your ability to see God at work.

You can set aside some time every day to meditate as well. Choose a portion of Scripture that you find meaningful. Read it once. Then read it again. Next, focus on a phrase or word that tells you something about God and repeat it over and over again. Let it sink deep into your consciousness. Meditate upon what this truth about God tells you about what God wants for you and from you. Think about others who may need to know what you are discovering about God and pray for them. Begin with just a few minutes and then challenge yourself to spend up to twenty minutes a day in such meditative prayer.

You can also use the Lord's Prayer for meditation. Pray the prayer and then stop and reflect on each phrase of the prayer. What does it tell you about God; about you; about God's will?

Meditation as a source of spiritual well-being has proven to have salutary affects on health in a number of studies. For example, the Franklin Cardiac Rehabilitation Program of Southwestern Community College did a study (Morris 2001) designed to investigate whether the scores from a questionnaire measuring spiritual well-being correlated with progression or regression of coronary heart disease. Participants in Dr. Dean Ornish's Lifestyle Heart Trial were given the "Spiritual Orientation Inventory" and a significant difference was found over a four year time period between the control group which did not engage in spiritual practices and a research group that practiced daily meditation.

The "spiritual orientation" scores of the two groups were significantly correlated with the degree of progression or regression of coronary artery obstruction. Those with low scores on the Spiritual Orientation Inventory had the most progression of coronary obstruction, while those with the highest scores had the most regression.

Daily prayer leads to growth in our spiritual health. We should not be at all surprised if a consequence of daily prayer is an improvement in physical health and emotional well-being. But that is not the intent. The intent is to grow into eternity (in the present moment) in relationship to Jesus Christ.

Weekly Worship. "You know, Pastor Mike, I don't come to church much. I can worship God better out hunting than in church," he said.

We had grown into a friendship based on our shared love of outdoors sports. We had hunted a couple of times and gone fishing together. Now we were talking about God and, though he acknowledged his belief in Jesus Christ, he didn't think church attendance was important.

I am convinced that the real power of corporate worship is that sacred moment when each person meets the Risen Savior within the communion of saints.

"Well," I began. "You know that I love the outdoors. The only problem I have with what you say is that I don't know what god you worship outdoors. Is it the god of the beautiful sunrise or the vicious god of the wolf that hunts and kills the rabbit?"

"What do you mean?" he asked.

"Well, it seems to me that one of the real benefits of attending church is that worship grounds us in the witness of scripture and the community of faith. When that happens, the chances are greater that we will encounter the real God wherever we are instead of the god we make up to fit our own ideas and desires. One of the reasons I feel so strongly about worship," I continued, "is that we can have greater confidence in the God we come to know in worship than in any god we think we are getting to know in other places. And that could make a difference when we need the real God, don't you think?"

I'd like to report that my friend changed his habits and worshiped weekly after that conversation. He didn't. But he did worship more frequently. Change sometimes takes time.

I have become an unabashed advocate for corporate worship. I am not naive. I know that one of the real problems with church today is that worship does not strike deeply into the heart of our people. I am constantly challenging myself and my staff to listen to what our worshipers are saying and then to respond with worship that is both spiritually deep and yet simple enough for anyone to enter into.

I am convinced that the real power of corporate worship is that sacred moment when each person meets the Risen Savior *within the communion of saints*. Everything in worship ought to serve that moment, the moment when what we pray and sing and say together shapes (and often transforms) our understanding of God and ourselves.

One of my favorite questions to ask about worship is this: What face do you put on God? Many people have unconsciously put a face on God that limits their relationship with God. For some the face of God is that of a demanding parent who always catches us in what we have done wrong or failed to do. Others see God as a kindly person who tolerates even the intolerable. Still others see God as a magician who magically changes life from bad to good. Some see Jesus, in particular, as a skillful teacher or a kind miracle worker. In each of these faces that we put on God, the character of God is limited.

If God is a demanding parent, there can be no peace in his presence and we are likely to feel only guilt or shame. If we see God as the epitome of tolerance, then we fail to grasp God's deep desire for justice—which is clearly intolerance for oppression—and are likely to be indifferent to human caused, unnecessary suffering. If the mask our God wears is that of a magician, we won't understand the God who refused to heal St. Paul in order to grow his faith, and we are likely to be disappointed when the "magic" doesn't work for us. If we see the face of Jesus as that of just a kindly miracle worker or teacher, then we are likely to ignore his call to serve others in love and share our financial wealth.

The real problem emerges when our limited picture of God collides with real life. In real life, only the God who alone is God—not the God of our imaginings—proves adequate. Corporate worship is the incubator for understanding this real God revealed in Jesus Christ through the Scriptures. This is the One who is wild enough, beyond us enough, and ultimately real enough to be worthy of our worship.

> The God made known most clearly in Jesus of Nazareth is beyond our ability to control or domesticate.

Our original sin (attempting to be like God) can easily take the form of making God in our own image. We need to "unlearn" our limited images of God so we can learn what it means for us to have been made in the image of the Holy Other. It is in worship—done well and fully participated in—where such unlearning and learning are facilitated. The god we make in our own image will always prove too small for our worship, too inadequate for our lives.

The God made known most clearly in Jesus of Nazareth is beyond our ability to control or domesticate. This is the God who has created the wild and wonderful diversity of our world. This is the God of quarks and black holes and an ever-expanding universe. This is the God of planets and suns, orbits and free flying comets. But this is

> Worship takes the neatness out of our spiritual lives by placing us in the presence of a God we cannot domesticate who calls us to follow Jesus in God's Way.

also the God who knows us better than we know ourselves. This is the God of grace who calls us to new beginnings by inviting us to own our stuff (confession) so that we can learn who we are in God and set the past in an appropriate context (forgiveness), and grow into forever. This is the God of justice, love, and mercy who, by the power of the Holy Spirit, transforms us into Christ-likeness and then calls us to bear Christ into the world.

The great benefit of corporate worship is our ongoing and cumulative exposure to the Truth of God. The Truth of God takes root within us through prayers and hymns, through scripture and sermon, through water, bread and wine, all while we sit next to someone we may love or dislike, may know or consider a stranger, may have sinned against or been sinned against by. Worship takes the neatness out of our spiritual lives by placing us in the presence of a God we cannot domesticate who calls us to *follow Jesus in God's Way.*

The person who says that they love God and yet does not regularly participate in corporate worship is like the man who says he loves his wife but never spends any real time with her getting to know her, letting her get to know him. In such a case, love is just an abstract idea with no power to either touch the life of the other or sustain the relationship when temptations come or life gets hard. And of course, when love is just an idea and not that deep experience of intimacy that comes from truly knowing another, there is no joy.

I remember the first time Joe returned to worship after months of battling a life threatening illness. He had been in and out of intensive care and now he slowly made his way home. The very next weekend he came limping on the strong arm of his wife down the center aisle of the church.

When I left the chancel to greet him, I asked him why he had rushed to come to church. His response startled me:

"No one could keep me away," he said. "I've come to thank God and this congregation for being with me and holding me up through everything. No one could keep me away."

He is one of my "weekly miracles," one of those who have overcome life difficulties and discovered the joy of weekly worship. Some are like my friend, Joe, whose struggle with poor health has been the catalyst. Others are women and men who have undergone the loss of children, or life-long careers, or financial security and, instead of railing against God and turning away in anger, have returned to worship because nothing could keep them away. My "weekly miracles" also include folks who seemingly have everything: strong family, wealth and prestige, good health, and yet they too have found worship in a community of faith to be a source of strength and an antidote to hubris and self-indulgence.

Human beings have been created with a need for God and one another. Corporate worship is the only event I know of that answers to both needs simultaneously. If this is true, then why is weekly worship on the decline?

I suspect there are many factors involved in this cultural phenomenon. Among them, American individualism. In our society we tend to confuse a personal relationship with God with a private relationship with God. There is, however, no biblical basis to affirm the notion of a private faith. Each disciple, though called personally, was called into a community. As long as we think Christianity condones a private faith, it is easy to deny our need for corporate worship.

After all, it seems so much simpler to believe by myself. I don't have to expose my faith to others nor deal with their shortcomings (or my own) in the context of our shared faith. Simpler, in this case, however, is not better. There is limited possibility for growth in a private faith.

On the other hand, both the inspiration and the irritation of others in worship can provoke us to examine ourselves and answer the invitation into a deeper, life-changing faith. Strength is the result of pushing against resistance. Worship strengthens our souls by engaging us in battling our own inner resistance to community in God's presence. Worship, while strengthening our souls, also improves the health of our bodies.

The remarkable consequence of communal interaction in God's presence is a statistically significant lowering of high blood pressure. According to a study (Gillum and Ingram 2006) by the National Center for Health and Statistics, in Hyattsville, Maryland: "Compared with never attending, attendance at religious services weekly or more than weekly was associated with somewhat lower adjusted hypertension prevalence and blood pressure in a large national survey." If you want to grow deep in Jesus Christ, worship is not optional.

Daily Bible Reading. My friend, John, served twice in Vietnam. During his second tour of duty, the expression "fragging" became a household word. Fragging means to kill one's own officer. John was an officer. He was sent to a post in the countryside of Vietnam with two orders: first, to purge his troops of the drugs and prostitution that were apparently rampant there and, second, to secure a local hill top for strategic purposes.

> The fruits of daily Bible reading include the courage to stand up for what ultimately matters and the willingness to face the consequences when we do.

John told me that there were times when he would walk the perimeter by himself and hear threats to his life called out in unidentifiable voices that were, he knew, his own troops. He would wake up at night to the sound of gunfire, never knowing if this time the gun would be aimed at him.

But he also told me how he could sleep under those incredibly stressful conditions. He showed me the little Bible that he carried with him and read every night. That Bible was for him tangible proof that, although he felt vulnerable and alone, God had neither deserted nor forgotten him. His Bible and the faith it nourished were the source of his confidence and courage.

The fruits of daily Bible reading include the courage to stand up for what ultimately matters and the willingness to face the consequences when we do. This was most certainly my friend, John's, experience. Throughout history, untold women and men of faith have faced threats, persecution, and even death with the courage and inner strength they gained from the Scriptures. My friend John survived his tours in Vietnam and his faith and personal courage have continued to grow as he continues to meet life head-on.

We live in a time when the courage and inner strength that daily Bible reading provides is vital. On the one hand, our faith will be tested in many ways. We face temptations that previous generations never knew. For example, access to mountains of information is as near as a click of the computer mouse and the Internet. The amount and extent of information that can be found on the Internet staggers the imagination and often challenges our moral sensibility. The World Wide Web can be used for good or for ill, for personal enhancement or detriment, for the betterment of others or their abuse. A firm grounding in the Bible provides a place to stand both when confronting temptation and when struggling with the complex moral challenges of our time.

On the other hand, simplistic faith, rigid dogma, religious fundamentalism, and judgmental attitudes promise a

false security in the face of our complex and often dangerous world. Faith based on the "authority" of someone else
and not on your own personal engagement with scripture
within the community of faith is dangerous. Meeting the
living Word in the written Word is the way through the
religious and social conundrums of our time.

"Pastor Mike," he said, "I've been attending a Bible
study at another church and I'm having some problems
with it. How can God tell the Israelites to go into Ai and
kill everyone: men, women and children? How does that
square with Jesus Christ?"

"Well, you're asking the right questions," I replied.
"We believe that, since Jesus is God's ultimate revelation
of who God is, we should test what is in the Bible by what
he taught, how he lived and acted. So, we could say that—
being finite and sinful people like the rest of us—those
who wrote the Bible may at times have misunderstood
God's intentions. Or they might well have projected their
own propensity to violence upon God in order to gain
divine sanction for it. We see that happening all the time.
At least these two options fit with the teaching of Jesus
that we should love our enemies and do good to those who
hate us" (Luke 6:27).

"Well, all I know is that it didn't make any sense to me.
I can't wait to get into the New Testament," he replied.

"That's great," I said. "But while you are reading the
Old Testament just remember that the God of Jesus is
the same God that acted again and again in the history of
Israel. So, watch for how and where God acts in the Old
Testament, judging in order to save, promising in order to
bring hope, and recreating in order to renew. Then, I think
you'll get it."

The problem many people have with reading the Bible
is that all too often the churches have neither encouraged

their questions nor affirmed them when they do ask questions. Like many pastors, I am embarrassed to say that for years I gave answers to questions no one was asking! The church and its pastors and teachers need to recognize that the Holy Spirit works in the lives of people who read the Bible. As Jesus said, "When the Spirit of truth comes, he will guide you into all the truth" (John 16:13). Anyone who trusts that will take the Bible very seriously as the doorway to wisdom.

> Although Jesus comes to us in many ways and the Spirit teaches us in many ways, pride of place goes to the Bible.

The eternal truth that Christians proclaim is found in the life, teachings, death, and resurrection of Jesus of Nazareth, the promised Messiah. Although Jesus comes to us in many ways and the Spirit teaches us in many ways, pride of place goes to the Bible. It is our foundational access point to the revelation of God in Jesus.

Sadly, with the rise of biblical illiteracy, the religious extremes and their spiritual fads seem to dominate the religious conversation in our country. In a time when works of fiction such as *The Da Vinci Code* become for countless people a primary source of information about who Jesus of Nazareth is, and what he did or didn't do, the critical task of the Church is to invite people into a deeper conversation on biblical truth.

To state the obvious, the crisis of biblical illiteracy will only end when Christians begin to read the Bible in the light of the questions that trouble and challenge them as they live and work in our complex world. Churches should make Bible literacy a theme and promote it and plan for it. Pastors and those who already read the Bible regularly need to be deliberate in enthusiastically encouraging those who don't to give it a try.

Something wondrous happens when we read the Bible regularly. Call it joy. Regular Bible reading leads to intimacy with God and there is great joy in great intimacy. For many people, beginning a regular reading of the Bible is their first awakening to a God who desires to speak directly to them. For those who have encountered this God, regular Bible reading deepens their relationship to God and opens them more and more to what God wants for them and what God wants from them.

When we read the Bible on a regular basis, the Holy Spirit takes the written Word and communicates the Risen Word, Jesus, in ways that meet the life circumstances we find ourselves in. Growing wisdom, faith, inner strength, courage, hope, and joy are among the many fruits of opening (and reading) the Holy Bible day after day.

One of the more embarrassing discoveries I made a number of years ago was that I had drifted away from a daily personal conversation with God through the Bible. I am not certain how it happened. I had entered seminary because I had been touched by the power of God's truth for me as I read the Scriptures. I loved all the academic tools and methods for interpreting the Bible but, along with studying the Bible, I still read it devotionally. After being in the ministry for five or six years, however, I woke up one day to discover that the only time I was reading the Bible was when preparing for a Bible study or sermon. And my spiritual well had run dry.

Not knowing how to recover my lost passion for the Bible, I simply began to read. Daily Bible reading is now a part of my life—not to prepare for what I may teach but in order to subject my spirit to the work of the Holy Spirit. I need that—and so do you.

I know that I am not alone. I have spoken to countless pastors and church workers, as well as ordinary Christians, who have shared the same experience. As they began to practice daily Bible reading for their own soul's delight, they have consistently reported a renewal of energy and commitment to the Gospel.

For those of us who have recovered our devotional use of Scripture it is much easier to trust the Holy Spirit to teach and guide others as they read the Bible. This openness to the spiritual journey of others as they read through the Bible themselves leads to profound dialogue, significant and challenging questions, and a deeper appreciation for and experience of the love that God communicates through the written Word.

> Daily Bible reading has the power to break down the walls we build between the secular and the sacred.

Many ordinary Christians—professionals, teachers, and laborers—discover in the Bible a new way of seeing their lives and the world. They reframe the circumstances of their lives by looking at them through the lens of Scripture. How they live is often radically transformed by the growing conviction that the God of Jesus, the God of Peter, James, John, and Paul, the God of Mary and Martha, Mary Magdalene, Lydia and Dorcas is meeting them and calling them to lives of similar significance. Daily Bible reading has the power to break down the walls we build between the secular and the sacred. The consequence is joy.

How do we begin? I have had many new Christians as well as life-long church attendees ask me which version of the Bible to buy. I suggest a recent translation—not a paraphrase unless the biblical language is simply inaccessible to them. I choose the *New Revised Standard Version* (NRSV) or the *New International Version* (NIV) more often than not. An edition of the Bible that has cross references, book introductions, study notes, concordance, and commentary can be helpful as well.

The next question I have heard at least as often is, "Where do I start?" I usually suggest either Luke's Gospel or the Gospel of Mark. Then a reading in Philippians or Colossians will often set the table for an excursion into Genesis and Exodus. When finished there, reading in the Psalms can be beneficial. I am confident that there are many ways to enter the Scriptures; in my experience these suggestions have simply met with great success in the lives of those seeking to develop a regular discipline of Bible reading.

I also encourage people not to get stopped by difficult passages or texts with which they simply cannot agree. My recommendation: pray over the passage and ask the Holy Spirit to teach you what you need to know. Stop and reflect and, if nothing comes, move on. The Bible is best interpreted in the whole, not by one passage in isolation from the rest.

I always suggest that, when moving through the Bible, disciples look for the God made known in Jesus in whatever they are reading. If you cannot see the God of Jesus in the text, I suggest you pray about it, trust the Spirit to make sense of it over time, and keep reading!

There are wonderful Bible classes available to enrich personal Bible reading. You can find commentaries on all the books of the Bible in religious and even secular bookstores. You can even find Internet Bible studies, commentaries, and chat rooms where Christians "talk" about the Bible. Nothing, however, can take the place of simply spending time by yourself and in a small group in God's Word.

Many years ago a wonderful man in the congregation I served was suddenly taken into the hospital. His blood pressure had spiked to 235 over 150. They couldn't bring it down with medication and so were forced to do emergency surgery. He survived the surgery only to lay in the hospital in delirium. The specialist that consulted with his wife said that it was likely he would never come out of it.

But his wife, who sat a vigil beside him, remarked how he would suddenly and very clearly repeat a psalm or other passage of Scripture. Or he would say the Lord's Prayer or the Apostles' Creed. She told me that she didn't think he had memorized any Bible verses, but there he was saying them.

After my friend came into his right mind, the specialist said that it was the closest thing to a miracle he had ever seen. When his wife shared how her husband had repeated Scripture and the Lord's Prayer, the specialist thought for a moment and then said, "You know, those may have been his only connection to this world. It's likely they brought him back."

What my friend's wife hadn't fully appreciated was the deep influence on her husband from reading the Bible and from hearing it read in worship for years. When he most needed it, the Holy Spirit seems to have used it to call him back to a life worth living.

Serving Others. My wife and I have taken Thanksgiving as an opportunity to serve beyond our local church. Since our children have gone (and when we were not spending that holiday with them) we have begun volunteering at the Salvation Army to serve the Thanksgiving meal.

One year when my cousin was the food director at the Salvation Army in the city, she asked if we could help serve the Thanksgiving meal and we leapt at the chance. We arrived early and had time to help set things up and then chat with my cousin, Ellen. More volunteers showed up than expected, and Ellen asked if my wife and I would greet people as they came in and make them feel welcome. We quickly agreed.

I remember extending my hand, smiling and welcoming the adults who were the first to enter. But the men and women would only look at the floor and then quietly say, "No, thank you." Then they moved quickly into the dining area. This continued until a family entered.

The first of this family to come to the dining hall was a little boy. I knelt down and, looking him in the eyes, welcomed him and told him how happy we were that he had come. And he smiled. Then, without thinking, I looked up at his father behind him who was smiling at his son. Extending my hand to the father, I welcomed him as well. And, for the first time that morning, an adult looked me in the eye and smiled.

> Serving is always about looking up at the ones we serve—not down on them.

Now I'm rather tall, but from that moment on I would bend down lower to make eye contact with those who came in—and invariably, they would smile in return. That little boy gave me a wonderful gift that Thanksgiving. I learned that serving is always about looking up at the ones we serve—not down on them.

There is a richness in life that simply cannot be attained unless we are willing to set our pride and position aside to serve others. That Thanksgiving Christine and I both received so much more than we had given in our serving. But it always works out that way in Christian service.

Human beings have been created with a need to serve. We are created, the Bible says, in the image of God. God is the original servant. The first act of serving in the Bible is

God's act of creation. Both accounts of creation in Genesis speak of God creating out of the sheer joy of creating itself. This joy is completed when humankind is placed in the midst of creation to discover and steward it. God's serving work in creation was then shared with God's children. Created in God's image, we cannot discover the best of who we are and can become until and unless we serve.

One of the most transforming events that I have seen in the lives of teens and adults is a mission trip. Whether it is helping to rebuild houses after the devastation of a hurricane like Katrina on the Gulf Coast or working with children in the Dominican Republic, no one returns home the same. I have watched men whose previous involvement in church was minimal, and for whom any emotional connection with religion was distant at best, tear up when sharing their experiences on a mission trip. I have had parents come up to me and express their profound gratitude for the life change in a teen who had returned from a mission trip to Appalachia or the Gulf Coast. When we get out of our comfort zones and go to where the need is great, when we cross cultural and class boundaries to serve people who need what we can offer, we discover that God is there ahead of us, calling us, blessing us, and blessing others through us.

When we serve, we see others differently. When we serve, we see our own lives differently. When we serve, our hearts open to the self-giving love of God in Jesus Christ. No wonder our lives are changed.

Service takes many forms. I believe we are all called to serve within our community of faith. This can be as simple as ushering at a worship service or as challenging as serving on the Church Council or teaching Sunday School. We can help in the kitchen for a church meal, rake leaves off the churchyard, and visit sick members of the congregation. We can collect food or clothing to be distributed through a community agency or by our own church. There are so many ways to serve God's people by serving in the church; the list is almost endless. Such serving opens our hearts to the wonder of our congregation's ministry and mission and connects us profoundly with the people we serve with.

The people who have the most difficulty seeing God at work in mission within the local church are those who are not involved—except to come and take. Disciples understand that the command of Christ to serve includes the sharing of our gifts, passions, and abilities in the local congregation.

Christian service, however, is not limited to service within the church. Beyond our local church, we serve when we reach out to meet the needs of the larger community around the church. God is at work in our lives when our personal ministry takes us to the local ball field to coach or referee a game, or when we serve as a Scout Master, on the local School Board, or in the Chamber of Commerce. When we serve a shelter meal, sort groceries at a food shelf, or mentor a struggling child, God is at work in our lives. When we advocate for justice, lobby our legislators on important social issues, stand up for those who cannot stand up for themselves, or give voice to the voiceless, God is at work in our lives.

Again, the list is endless. God didn't create us to be uninvolved! God created us with the capacity to love; service is love in action. Or to quote Paul again, service is "faith working through love" (Galatians 5:6).

When I have been asked how to start serving by those who have never done it, I simply encourage them to find an area of interest and simply show up. Talk to your pastor or drop in at one or more local social service agencies. Find out what needs to be done and help do it. Finally, there is no way to serve except to serve.

Relate to Others for Spiritual Growth. "Pastor, I think I finally understand this *relate to others for spiritual growth* stuff."

Smiling, I replied, "Don't tell me you finally joined a small group, John?"

"Are you kidding?!" he scoffed. "I don't have time for that—though I am sure it would be a good idea." This, of course, was in consideration for our friendship.

"No, what I mean is that since I've been at this discipleship stuff," he continued, "I can't treat my employees the same way I used to. I mean, I always tried to treat them fairly, that wasn't an issue. It's just that, well I see them differently. I hate to admit it, but I value them more now. That's all."

That wonderful businessman taught me something in that conversation. When spiritual relationships became an important part of my life it was in a small group. In small groups, my wife and I have grown, shared our deepest concerns and most difficult transitions, and made great faith friends. Conversely, when we have not had a small group of friends for prayer and sharing we have experienced both loneliness and a deeper hunger for relationships that work.

This isn't surprising. After all, we have been created for relationship. Research by Thomas Lewis, Fari Amini and Richard Lannon in their groundbreaking book, *A General Theory of Love* (2001), has suggested that love (meaningful relationship) is physically necessary for human beings. What has been consistently shown is that human beings are happiest around other people.

> Relating to others for spiritual growth not only has great impact on how we treat other people; it changes how we see ourselves.

Harvard University researcher Edward O. Wilson has called this the "biophilia hypothesis," an assertion that living things yearn for proximity to other living things:

> On the whole married people are happier than singles, people in large families are happier than those in small families, those who are busy and attend lots of events where they interact with other people are happier than those who hang around the house. Research finds that a person is more likely to feel happy in a friends-or-family social setting than when alone." (Easterbrook 2004)

No wonder, in a fast paced and endlessly changing time, small groups in churches have become an underground social movement. People hunger for real, enduring relationships with people they can learn to trust and with whom they can share deeply all the joys and sorrows that life brings them. Churches that have built small groups into the fabric of their ministries are meeting a deep seated human need for connections—and their ministries are growing while others are in decline.

The power of seeing relationships as spiritual encounters (a vision that emerges within small groups) changes how we see and value others. Once again, we ought not be surprised. When we experience joy in our lives, we naturally take it into every aspect of our living. Conversely, when we are lonely or disheartened these feelings color how we interact with others as well as how we interpret those interactions. We all know this, but now research has powerfully confirmed it. Relating to others for spiritual growth not only has great impact on how we treat other people; it changes how we see ourselves.

"I love coming to church," Ron said. "I drive forty minutes one way on Sundays to come to worship because it changes my outlook. No matter how difficult the week has been, no matter how many contracts I may have lost or how many customers have yelled at me, I feel better about myself," he continued, "and I treat my family better."

I smiled and said how glad I was that he was willing to drive so far to come to church. It was clergy-speak for not knowing what to say.

"No. You don't understand," Ron replied. "My wife, who goes to another church, often turns to me when I've been grouchy or just plain difficult and will say, 'It's time you went to church, Ron.' And she's right! Being with the people at church, connecting again with God and my friends there, makes all the difference in the world."

What Ron and his wife understood was that the relationships he had established and maintains through weekly worship change how he feels about himself. This inner renewal through worship was visible to his wife and, I suspect, the rest of his family. He works in his home office and his wife works away from the home. His days can be spent in intense work in isolation from others. Relationships that are founded on spiritual values are critical to his well-being.

With the research and the experience in ministry that I have had, I find it not at all surprising that the growing percentage of non-worshipers in our society parallels the rise of depression. Gregg Easterbrook (2004) writes: "In 1957, 3 percent of Americans described themselves as 'lonely.' Today 13 percent do." While other mitigating factors are surely involved (better diagnosis and better treatment among them) the parallel between declining worship population and increasing depression is striking.

There are two ways we can choose to find relationships that grow our sense of value for ourselves and for others. The first is to find a place of worship and get involved in an activity. This will need to be an opportunity to work with others, not by yourself. It should also be a regular activity in which people will recognize when you are present as well as when you are absent. For men it can be a "fix it" group, a men's Bible study or prayer group, a social service project, or any other regularly scheduled group where relationships can be built naturally. Men often have more difficulty getting involved in the ministries of the church. If there aren't groups like these in your church, start them.

Women have more opportunities in many of our churches through women's groups and ministries. (Of course, there are women who would love to be part of a "fix it" group too!) The point is to find an activity where you will feel comfortable about what you are doing so that you can move beyond your discomfort in being with people you don't yet know. Don't try to join groups where you have no interests or skills. Find a group that engages your passions and abilities and you will be more likely to hang in there, make great relationships, and accomplish great things in the ministry and mission of God's church.

Another way to find relationships is to go on a mission trip. The shared experience of going somewhere to help others in need will create a deep sense of community and lasting friendships—both with members of the mission team and with those you go to serve. It is a profound experience. Mission trips often lead to reunion events that continue to nurture and deepen the relationships established on the trip.

Relating to others for spiritual growth is really about health, our own health as well as the health of our churches and communities. The more we feel valued and truly strive to value others, the greater the experience of shared joy.

Give Generously. As the poet, Elizabeth Bibesco, said: "Blessed are those who can give without remembering and take without forgetting" (Wallace, 1983).

Generosity is not natural to human beings. It is taught. If we watch a group of small children playing, it is most frequently about protecting my toy or my space. We naturally cling to what we have. Sharing is a learned behavior.

"I have something to give you," he said.

We were sharing lunch together and he had a wide grin on his face. Then he handed me a check for $50,000. I remember stammering my thanks on behalf of myself and the church. But he waved it away and continued: "No, thank you. My wife and I are so thankful that we can give and the ministry of the church means so much to us. We only wished we could give more."

Then, with a twinkle in his eye, he said, "Someday I want to write a check to the church with six figures."

I remember sharing that event with my wife, Christine. That's when I told her that someday I'd love to write a check with five figures to the church. And someday I will!

Generosity is contagious. We have to be exposed to it in order for it to penetrate our resistance to giving. Unless we are exposed to the joy of generosity we will naturally think of our financial giving as loss instead of gain. The tragedy is that most of us are far more concerned about what we do not have than what we do have and ought to share.

When we cling to what we have we close our hearts to joy. The generosity of God is in our spiritual DNA, but it must be awak- Generosity springs from the heart of gratitude. Gratitude is the attitude of joy.

ened. When generosity is awakened the result is joy—a joy that cannot be imagined until experienced. When generosity is stifled or held in check, we live under a regrettable pall of selfishness—and there is no joy there.

I have met many misers in my life. I have yet to meet one who is happy. Conversely, I have met many generous souls, all of whom had a spirit of joy that was tangible. Generosity springs from the heart of gratitude. Gratitude is the attitude of joy.

When the divine spirit of giving within us is awakened and set loose, gratitude to God for all we have and are able to do bubbles up from the depths of our souls. Generosity, we come to see, is a giving back from what we have been given.

My friend was absolutely serious when he told me he had the goal of writing a check to the church in six figures. My wife and I have grown in the joy of giving and have written checks in four figures. Our goal of writing a five figure check hasn't been reached yet, but we are well into the four figures range each year. As we have grown in our giving, we have discovered an incredible spiritual truth: You can't out-give God.

When we discovered that we couldn't out-give God, we discovered it wasn't about money. A sacrificial gift is just that—a gift of money (or time) that requires giving up other things. The gift we receive back from God is not more money to cover the sacrifice but a divine blessing of the soul that is very real. Over and over again our God has more than matched our financial giving with blessings we could not have imagined.

And our attitude toward money has changed. We still strive to manage our financial resources well—that's just good stewardship. But we now live as though money is *just one* (and not the most important) *of our resources*. The result is an unexpected freedom to give. You can't out-give God—but I like to challenge people to try. There is great joy in trying!

The second tragedy I have seen is that when we are consumed with worry about what we don't have, or whether we have enough, we don't talk together about what we do have and how we can invest it in life. In families this means that our children are not exposed to the joy of generosity and miss out on the chance to have this "fruit of the Spirit" (Galatians 5:22) cultivated within them. As they grow and enter our acquisitive, consumerist culture, discovering the joy of giving on their own will be very difficult—not impossible, but difficult. When we overly safe-guard our possessions, we are not likely to talk about them and the good they might do if we shared them. Instead of modeling (for our children and others) responsible and joyful giving, no matter what we say we model selfishness—which is definitely not one of the "fruits of the Spirit."

I urge people to give with generous and grateful hearts and to talk about it with their families. Children should be a part of the decision-making when their parents choose where to give. More than that I encourage an allowance for children from which a tenth should be set aside to give away in service to others and a tenth should be invested in their own future through savings. And we need to make sure that our children see the positive results in the lives of others that come from the family's giving.

> The only reason any child or adult goes hungry in our country (and in the world) is that our abundance has simply not been shared.

Provision for our tomorrows cannot be at the expense of our generosity today. We need to teach our children the discipline of giving, celebrate it with them, and then watch as they reap the joy that comes from generous living.

Perhaps the greatest tragedy of clinging to what we have is the negative impact on our society and world.

The only reason any child or adult goes hungry in our country (and in the world) is that our abundance has simply not been shared. God has created and sustains the world in such a way as to be bountiful enough to feed every man, woman and child. But our political greed and unwillingness to share for fear that it will diminish our standard of living has led to hunger and privation that is unnecessary.

As a people Americans tend to be generous in times of catastrophe and crisis at home and abroad. If we paid attention we would see that in spite of our giving, our standard of living continues to rise. We could do so much more and still have more than we need.

The generosity of individuals can lead to generosity of the nation. When hurricane Katrina slammed into the Gulf Coast states, our national government proved ineffective in its response to the enormous tragedy we witnessed on our television screens. In spite of the government's ineptness, the people of the United States responded with an outpouring of generosity *The more willing we are to give generously, the greater the happiness and sense of having helped create a better world.* that was nothing short of miraculous! In fact, the giving was so great and so fast, that we couldn't get the resources to where they were needed as quickly as they were given. The generosity of individual Americans clearly communicated an expectation that a similar and effective generosity would be developed on the federal level.

As the debate about global warming heats up, our expectations for individual, local, regional, national and global responses will include a demand for—and a willingness to—sacrifice for the future of our children and grandchildren—indeed, for all of the world's children and grandchildren. Generosity creates more of its kind; selfishness does the same.

The promise of God is clear. The prophet Malachi writes:

> Will anyone rob God? Yet you are robbing me! But you say, "How are we robbing you?" In your tithes and offerings! You are cursed with a curse, for you are robbing me—the whole nation of you! Bring the full tithe into the storehouse, so that there may be food in my house and thus put me to the test, says the Lord of hosts; see if I will not open the widows of heaven for you and pour down for you an overflowing blessing.... Then all nations will count you happy, for you will be a land of delight, says the Lord of hosts. (Malachi 3:8-10, 12)

The power of this text goes far beyond its religious implications. We see, in fact, that the curse of selfishness is a lack of joy. There is little delight in the hearts of that person or that nation that cannot share from its abundance. Conversely, the more willing we are to give generously, the greater the happiness and sense of having helped create a better world. The Word of God in Malachi is a word for anyone who seeks to discover true joy in this life—quite apart from any eternal ramifications.

How do we begin? First, take an honest look at what you have given in the past year. When you add it all up, how close to 10% of your take-home pay is it? Then make a commitment to close that gap. Set a goal of reaching a tithe (ten percent of take-home pay) over the next year or so. If you are at a low percentage, it may take you more than two or three years to get to a tithe. But discipline yourself and get there. You'll find joy on the other side of faithful tithing.

Then look for those opportunities to give beyond your plan or to give more than your tithe if you've already reached that level. These can be your moments of sacrificial giving. Remember—the offering begins when the tithe is given. Sacrificial giving is a response of the heart, in faith, to an extraordinary need. I have found that such giving, along with meeting those extraordinary needs, creates an inner sense of well-being that is remarkable.

The only way to start is simply to start. Create your giving plan (with your family if you are married). Write it down and keep it in a place where you can look at it when you need to. Make your goal a percentage, instead of a dollar amount, so that whatever changes you experience in your income you can naturally adjust to them. Then, for your own sake, make a good faith estimate of what an amount, based on today's real income, might be. Pray over it (with your family) and then start.

Remember: you can't out-give God—but you should try!

QUESTIONS FOR FURTHER REFLECTION

What place does prayer have in your life right now? What steps might you take to integrate prayer more fully in your life? Commit now to taking those steps and get started.

What, if any, are your obstacles to worshiping weekly? What steps can you take to overcome those obstacles? Commit now to taking those steps and get started.

Do you read the Bible every day? If not, why not? Commit now to reading the Gospels (Matthew, Mark, Luke, and John) in the next 30 days (about 3 pages a day) and get started.

❧ What does it feel like to think about going out of your comfort zone to serve others? God goes with you when you travel outside your comfort zone for love so pick a project and get started.

❧ Think of the relationships within which you and your partner both experience spiritual growth. What steps might you take to strengthen those relationships? Commit now to taking those steps and get started.

❧ What percentage of your net income do you presently give either to your church or to organizations that serve the needs of the disadvantaged? Make a plan to get you to ten percent as soon as possible and get started.

CHAPTER FIVE

Learning Life's Greatest Lessons

Life experience taught Booker T. Washington that: "Success is to be measured not so much by the position that one has reached in life as by the obstacles which he has overcome while trying to succeed" (Wallace 1983). I have seen the truth of Washington's wisdom many times.

"If you could share about the things that matter the most to you, what would you share with us?"

The question took me by surprise. I was meeting with a group of pastors. We had gathered at a retreat house in Indiana to discuss ministry that works. The conversation had touched on care of people, discipleship, and the challenges of growing a community of faith. Then, in the afternoon of the last day, one of my colleagues asked me that question. I don't know how I replied. But I have lived with the question ever since.

The question, of course, is one that demands the deepest reflection we can give. It expects us to prioritize life's lessons and then respond. Frankly, having never faced such a question, I was unprepared for it. I suspect most of us would be. So I invite you to join me in considering three of life's greatest lessons that I have learned.

I hope that you will find it meaningful and stimulating enough so that you might begin your own list of life's greatest lessons—lessons you have learned, lessons you have yet to learn. The underlying conviction that disciples of Jesus share is that this life is eternity's playground (or perhaps we should say classroom).

God is up to something in and through our lives. Figuring out what it is and learning what God would have us learn should be the top priority of our lives. One of the joys of discipleship is personal growth and wisdom. All the great lessons of life contribute to the deep joy that fills the lives of those who truly follow Jesus. So let's consider some of the lessons learned by living.

ACHIEVEMENT

Over the years I have been struck by how varied and personal the sense of achievement is. Some think it is related to their life's work. Others see it as the legacy they will leave behind which may have nothing to do with their life's work. Achievement is ultimately about significance and how each person evaluates her or his life.

At the very end of his life, my father said that it had all been worthwhile because "I have given birth to four sons who have turned out O.K. and, through them, a lot of grandchildren that I am proud to know."

It was a shocking revelation to me. I remembered my father and mother struggling to just make ends meet as they worked to provide for a family of four boys. My father was a laborer. He worked at the same job for over forty years. He went through coronary by-pass surgery, a number of angioplasty procedures, and finally met his match in lung cancer. At the end of his life, it wasn't the house he had paid off, nor the consistency of employment, nor even the many luxuries that he could finally afford that defined his life. His life achievement was in his sons and the ethical base that he had left in them—and through them in others.

On the other hand, I have a friend who has done very well in business. Yet, when I asked him about his achievements, he shared that the great achievement of his life was not his thriving business but the generosity that moves him to share the fruit of his success. He looks at the blessings that our God has given him and is thankful that all he has achieved makes possible his giving back to others.

In the years of ministry that I have had the privilege of serving, as well as the years of hospice care that I was able to participate in, I have never heard anyone glory in the achievement of financial success. One of life's greatest lessons is that we ought not wait. We ought to invest our lives in what truly matters to us today. Not that some could not have done so. On the contrary, I have had the privilege of serving some very successful people of all walks of life but invariably the great achievements that they claim at the end of their lives have little or nothing to do with worldly success. In every case it had to do with that subjective reality we call "legacy." What will I leave behind in this life that has made it all worthwhile?

That's why I love the quote from Booker T. Washington. He understood that the great achievements in life are the result of our triumphs over great obstacles. In my father's experience it was the overcoming of poverty that allowed him to provide for his family and the result-ing success of his sons that made it all worthwhile. The last thing my father said to me was this: "I've had a good life. I wouldn't have done it any differently." This from a man whose life was characterized by struggle—and by the achievement of what mattered most to him. I have not forgotten the joy that my father radiated when he shared that with me. And it had nothing to do with how others might have viewed his life. I have found that the opinions of others ultimately do not matter in the final analysis of one's life.

One of life's greatest lessons for me has been learned at the bedside of the dying. We spend so much time wooing the praise of others, but at the end of our lives such praise has no real value. What finally matters is being able to look back on the significance of our relationships—on love that has been given, and on obstacles that have been overcome for the sake of those relationships.

One of my personal heroes is Abraham Lincoln. He was an unlikely man to be elected president. The list of his obstacles is daunting, yet he overcame much and in the process forged the character and will that kept our country united. Here is a list of the obstacles he faced on the road to the White House:

Failed in business in 1831.
Defeated for Legislature in 1832.
Second failure in business in 1833.
Suffers nervous breakdown in 1836.
Defeated for Speaker in 1838.
Defeated for Elector in 1840.
Defeated for Congress in 1843.
Defeated for Congress in 1848.
Defeated for Senate in 1855.
Defeated for Vice President in 1856.
Defeated for Senate in 1858.
Elected President of the United States in 1860.

The great question in life is not what will happen to us, but what we will make of what happens to us. There are great men like Abraham Lincoln who teach us that. But there are also the unknown greats like my father and that Christian businessman who could teach us the same lesson.

My friend, the generous businessman, had faced a personal and professional crisis when the store in which he first started was closing his branch. Instead of taking a defeatist attitude and simply walking away, he was inspired by a friend to dream of what he could make of himself, and that opened the door to his success in business.

Achievement is the gift of God that springs from the personal hopes within us and the persistence to make them happen. What has astonished me is the vast witness of women and men who speak of life achievement in terms of the wealth of love and friendships. Achievement is, therefore, the end result of succeeding in what really matters.

One of life's greatest lessons is that we ought not wait. We ought to invest our lives in what truly matters to us today.

> Jesus looked up and saw rich people putting their gifts into the treasury; he also saw a poor widow put in two small copper coins. He said, "Truly, I tell you, this poor widow has put in more than all of them; for all of them have contributed out of their abundance, but she out of her poverty has put in all she had to live on." (Luke 21:1-4)

One of the great lessons of life is that achievement comes when we invest in forever—that's what the poor widow did in the text. Yes, it is about sacrifice. We cannot give to everything at the same time. We can (and should), like the widow, invest in what will ultimately matter. Her investment in eternity was commended by the Lord. A similar sacrifice for gambling would not have been affirmed. The sacrifice itself was not noteworthy. People then, as now, make sacrifices all the time. But she made her sacrifice for the sake of eternal purpose. She didn't wait until her fortunes had changed. She didn't wait until it would be easy to give. She gave for what she believed in.

Ultimately, that will define achievement for you and me. When it all comes down to it, will we look at our lives and judge that we sacrificed, gave up other things, took on tasks and responsibilities for what we judged truly mattered? What truly matters? When we can answer these questions, we can define achievement for ourselves.

BEAUTY AND LOVE

"I'm tired of it," he said with a sigh. "I'm tired of the dating scene and the expectations that come with it. And, Pastor Mike, I didn't know who else to talk to about it. So I've come to you."

I listened as this young man shared his frustrations. He had not found a life partner and was despairing of doing so. But what he then said shocked me.

"I have had my share of sexual partners, and if that's all there is to this stuff, then I'm done with it. I just want to meet a woman who can be my friend and not think that just because I choose not to go to bed with her I'm rejecting her or that something is wrong with me. What I want is more than that. Is that so strange?"

"It sounds like you want a real relationship, not just the shadow of one," I said. "I want to encourage you to do two things. The first is not to give up. I can tell you of conversations with wonderful women who would love to meet an attractive guy like you who believes what you just said!" I couldn't help laughing.

"But I also want to tell you not to give up on what you dream for. I believe that if you don't compromise you'll find her. Or, more appropriately, God will bless you and you'll find each other."

And two years later that's just what happened.

In the western world we seem to have lost sight of beauty. Where once we celebrated art as the gift of the sublime, we now have replaced it with the merely erotic or mundane. Surely the erotic and the mundane are part of the fabric of life, and to the degree that they are truly depicted, art sets a part of the human landscape before us. But there is little that is elevating about them.

> I just believe that within each of us beats a heart that drives for the greater rather than the lesser, the truly beautiful instead of the easy and cheap.

I'm neither prudish nor elitist. I don't blush at sexual innuendos nor am I oblivious to the ordinariness of life. I just believe that within each of us beats a heart that drives for the greater rather than the lesser, the truly beautiful instead of the easy and cheap.

One of the great spiritual life lessons available to each of us is that we should never surrender our ideals; they often define the truly beautiful that we long for.

That young man's ideal of a life partner, in every sense of that word, called him to a relationship that he could call beautiful and a love that can be called real. In our sexually permissive era, I keep hearing more and more of our young people saying that they want something more, something better—something beautiful.

"Isn't she beautiful?" he asked. My friend and I were at a dinner party and a lull in the conversation we were having led him to look away and then say these words to me. I followed his glance and saw that he was looking at his wife, an attractive middle-aged woman in a bright outfit with a cane beneath the chair on which she sat. She was laughing in an animated conversation with another member of our church. Crippling arthritis had stolen her mobility from her, but she had refused to allow it to shrink her world to the size and safety of her own home. Instead, she struggled to stay connected to her family, friends, and church.

"Yes," I replied, "She is."

He turned to me as if startled by my response. Then he said, "I really didn't know what courage was until I watched her handle this stuff. Now, I know." Then looking again in his wife's direction, he smiled and said, "Isn't she lovely?"

There is a beauty that only emerges over time. It is the beauty of the soul. This is the grandeur of a life that makes the difficult choice not to be defeated by illness, or debilitating disease, or the other trials and tribulations that life might bring. When that choice is made and lived in, loveliness grows in the soul and becomes visible.

Looking back on that conversation, I am not certain where the real beauty was. I knew her well enough to know that her decision to keep going out and connecting with people was not an easy one. I knew him well enough to know that caring for her and making it possible for her to do so was not always easy. The real beauty, I have come to believe, is in their relationship.

Love is the beauty they share. A real life, hard won but beautiful love that has stood the tests of time, is what they share.

St. Paul had it right:

If I speak in the tongues of mortals and of angels, but do not have love, I am a noisy gong or a clanging cymbal. And if I have prophetic powers, and understand all mysteries and all knowledge, and if I have all faith, so as to remove mountains, but do not have love, I am nothing. If I give away all my possessions, and if I hand over my body so that I may boast, but do not have love, I gain nothing.

Love is patient and kind; love is not envious nor boastful or arrogant or rude. It does not insist on its own way; it is not irritable or resentful; it does not rejoice in wrongdoing, but rejoices in the truth. It bears all things, believes all things, hopes all things, endures all things. Love never ends. (1 Corinthians 13:1-8a)

Whatever beauty is, it calls forth the best in us and elicits joy. Followers of Jesus understand that beauty is an ideal that is ultimately defined by love. Not love as a feeling, but love that works, love that endures because it never gives up on the other or the relationship. Perhaps our ability to appreciate and produce the beautiful in art and in love is also a part of our being created in the image of God.

I know it doesn't happen all the time. I understand that relationships between husbands and wives are sometimes broken. I fully know how lovers can lose their passion and their love. But the human heart still longs (and always will) for love that is beautiful and lasts. The divorce rate may be high in the United States, but the marriage rate continues unabated, all because our souls long for the love of which Paul wrote to be born within our real relationships.

My wife and I stood in a long line to view Da Vinci's masterpiece, the *Mona Lisa*. When we finally stood a few feet away from that great work of art, it dawned on me that she's not necessarily beautiful in a physical sense. Throughout the centuries, however, men and women have marveled at a mysterious inner and eternal beauty that subtly captures us in her small smile. It's that smile that invites us to gaze on an otherwise ordinary portrait.

Real beauty is like that smile. It takes the ordinary and elevates it to the extraordinary. True beauty is subtle, not obvious. In its very subtlety, it invites us to stop and wonder, just as the *Mona Lisa's* smile does.

God has given human beings the unique gift of seeing and appreciating, and even creating beauty. We know of no other creature who has this capacity. Perhaps our ability to appreciate and produce the beautiful in art and in love is also a part of our being created in the image of God. In any case, it is a fountain of joy for which we long and from which we experience depth and breadth in life.

LOSS AND GAIN

Henry Ward Beecher learned one of life's more important lessons: "God asks no man [or woman] whether [they] will accept life. That is not the choice. You must take it. The only choice is how" (Wallace 1983).

When my mother suddenly died, I flew to my boyhood home in Richland, Washington, to meet my father, brothers and their families. Having worked in hospice I had learned much about the processes of grief and mourning. I also knew that this was personal. This was not another's grief I had the privilege to share. This was mine.

I remember telling myself on the plane to feel my loss. The temptation to "professionalize" it, to make it into a pastoral lesson, was great. My way of resisting the temptation to deny my loss was to insist that I feel it. Of course, in the first hours and days of grief a numbness sets in, and so, in those early days, deeply feeling one's loss is difficult at best. That was my experience, but over the next year I felt and reflected and learned.

Grief is not a single event. It comes in waves. The emotional experience of each wave can be everything from anger to sorrow to guilt at what was never said or done and cannot now be said or done. Along with the bitter-sweet memories of love shared there is both the joy of knowing your loved one is with God and the emptiness of knowing he or she is not with you. Through these successive waves

I learned that loss can create wonderful gain—not immediately, but over time.

With the unexpected loss of my mother, I found myself clinging emotionally to those I loved. I felt an unconscious anxiety that would surprise me when I watched my teenaged daughters drive off to one of their many High School activities. My wife would be a little late and I'd begin to fret, only to find out later that the traffic had been unusually heavy.

One evening as I waited for the return of my daughters from another evening activity, I found myself worrying. I looked at my wristwatch and discovered that they weren't late. I stopped and asked God what he was trying to teach me in my anxiety.

My mind went back to my mother's death. Her loss brought back memories of how we had grown closer over the last few years before her death. I remembered how often we would talk with one another—almost every Sunday night. I thought of how I would always end our conversa- Love seeks the best for the other and the best we can give our families and friends is guidance and space to become all that God created them to be.

tions the same way: "I love you Mom." Except for that one Sunday when she didn't feel well and needed to get off the phone, and I was tired from an extended day of church activities. The night she died.

And I realized then that life is not hanging onto those we love. It is ultimately about treasuring them and letting them go. We treasure our loved ones by spending time with them—not by controlling them. We share ourselves and life with them while letting them go (in our love) to live their own lives.

It is simply impossible to live with joy if you are constantly fretting over how tenuous life is. It is not treasuring your loved ones to hold them so tight that you stifle your joy in them and their joy in you. To treasure those we love is to love those we treasure. Love seeks the best for the other, and the best we can give our families and friends is guidance and space to become all that God created them to be. I want those I love to know that's how I want to be—and try to be—for them. If they know that and I know that, then the inevitable disappointments and momentary surliness that can creep into any relationship will be placed in a much larger context. This is "how" I choose to take life.

When it comes to loss and gain, we need to remember, as difficult as it may be, that gain comes from letting go, from accepting our losses. For the person of faith, letting go is a profound act of trust. We trust the God who has created us and loves us, and let us go into our own lives. We trust those whom we love into that eternal love that we have experienced, whether they have seen the invisible hand of God in their moments and days or not. Letting go is an act of love.

She came to the altar for communion and was crying. In sharing the bread with her, I simply took her hand and held it silently for a moment in prayer. A widow, she is locked in the prison of her own grief. Having deeply loved her husband, his sudden death was an earthquake of the soul for her. The aftershocks have continued now for years. So she weeps. She tells others of her grief in an almost random manner. Her loss is the morning sun and the night stars.

She thinks that her grief is love. It is not. Her grief has become a tragic nostalgia. She clings to her memories of him without realizing that she is distorting the real love they shared. She no longer remembers him or even loves him; she loves the illusion her memories have put in his place.

Love is letting go. The act of letting go honors the relationships of the past without embalming us in them. Real love always sets us (and those we love) free for life, even in our losses.

The great act of God's love was a letting go: "God's love was revealed among us in this way: God sent his only Son into the world so that we might live through him (1 John 4:9). God's love took shape in our Creator's letting go of the Son to bring eternal love into the world.

One of life's greatest lessons is that we love best when we treasure and let go of those we love most. I would not have known this unless I had experienced both the loss of my mother, and the anxiety of losing my wife and daughters. The gain that comes from loss is a deep wisdom that opens our lives to letting go and trusting love.

> I have learned that loss is a personal and sacred journey that each of us will have to make in this life. If we are open, through faith, the journey will take us to the very edge of forever.

I don't judge this woman of faith in her prison of unresolved grief. Instead I hurt for her. I pray that she will be set free from her prison of feelings and mistaken memories. I pray for an event of love in her life again that will redefine her and help her reframe her life.

Dr. Lee Griffin, a Christian psychiatrist, used to say, "All life learning comes from pain. The tragedy is that not all pain leads to learning." I understood him to say that life's great lessons come when we can reflect on our painful experiences and allow the Holy Spirit to teach us.

Tragedy, pain, and challenge cannot teach us in and of themselves. Our ability to prayerfully reflect upon such experiences creates an opportunity for the Spirit to open us to see them in an eternal perspective. Without such a perspective joy quickly fades. With such a perspective joy will see us through.

After my mother's death I discovered a depth of empathy for those suffering loss that I had not experienced before. I had always been told that I was an effective caregiver in grief situations. Now there was, quite simply, an added dimension to my care. I listened more and without the need to provide answers. I realized that my caring presence was often the best, and sometimes the only, gift that I could bring to those experiencing great loss.

I have learned that loss is a personal and sacred journey that each of us will have to make in this life. If we are open, through faith, the journey will take us to the very edge of forever. Good Friday was, after all, the horizon of death. Though no one could see it, Easter was just over that vista. Just out of sight, to be sure, but real nonetheless.

There are few things that I have real confidence in. Life after death is one of them. This is the great gain we have received from God's great loss in letting the Son go all the way to the cross.

Disciples of Jesus Christ experience joy when this hope is realized in their own seasons of loss. We let go into a forever that our Savior has already entered. Death is no longer the great thief of life. Through the resurrection of Jesus Christ, God has tamed death. That grim specter is merely an usher sent to escort us into eternity.

Without this hope, all loss is just loss. With confidence in the promises of our faith, loss is gain. St. Paul writes:

> Yet, whatever gains I had, these I have come to regard as loss because of Christ. More than that, I regard everything as loss because of the surpassing value of knowing Christ Jesus my Lord. For his sake I have suffered the loss of all things, and I regard them as

rubbish, in order that I may gain Christ and be found in him. . . . (Philippians 3:7-8)

On the other side of loss is the greatest lesson of life—this life is forever's playground.

QUESTIONS FOR FURTHER REFLECTION

❧ What kind of legacy would you like to leave behind you?

❧ What steps do you need to take now to leave such a legacy behind you?

❧ In what ways do you both recognize and create beauty in your life?

❧ What significant losses have you experienced in your life?

❧ How did you react to those losses and what did your grief feel like?

❧ As you reflect on your experiences of loss, what gains do you think you have experienced as a result of those losses?

CHAPTER SIX

Don't Let Anything
Get in Your Way

"All you've got to do is get them involved in just one thing. Then you've got them hooked," he said with a grin. "The point is that there are always so many things that a person can do. But you can only do one at a time. That's the key—get them involved in just one thing at one time and they'll grow. I know," he continued, "that's what happened to me."

My friend and I were talking about his growing involvement in both the local congregation as well as overseas mission work. He had helped start a Christian school in an island nation, developed a fruit plantation there, and his fruits are now being sold to benefit a number of charitable organizations. He will tell you that discipleship has changed his life by wonderfully complicating it with joy and significance.

As a business man he has seen human need up close and personal; as a Christian he began feeling the Holy Spirit drawing him into action to meet those needs. He was willing to act, to step out in faith that God would lead, but sensed that he needed to spiritually prepare himself for service. He began to practice the *Marks of Discipleship*. That's where it all needs to start. We need to get our own spiritual lives in order if we are going to be effective in responding to the call of God to significance and purpose.

As my friend felt himself more and more empowered through practicing the *Marks of Discipleship*, he had the vision of empowering others through a Christian school. He grasped the opportunity to do so and the school became a reality.

One thing led to another and soon he purchased land. His purpose? To plant fruit trees as a commercial venture in which he could employ poverty stricken workers so they could support their families and their children could go to school. He had grasped another opportunity.

The next step was to export his fruit to the United States and find a market for it. What a remarkable moment it was when he discovered that he could sell his fruit through a charitable organization in the United States. Great good was accomplished on both sides of the ocean!

It all started with the first step. The first step springs from a willing heart. God will unlock the depths of eternal love for you and me if we are only willing to seek God's presence and be open to the Spirit's transforming work. Our part is only a willing heart.

OBSTACLES TO A WILLING HEART

There are, however, blocks that can close the willing heart. The disciple who seeks the joy of the Savior needs to be aware of some of these so that she/he can continue this spiritual journey we call life with purpose. Jesus teaches us about one of these blocks in the parable of the servants.

> For it is as if a man, going on a journey, summoned his slaves and entrusted his property to them; to one he gave five talents, to another two, to another one, *to each according to his ability.* Then he went away. The one who had received the five talents went off at once and traded with them, and made five more talents. In the same way, the one who had the two talents made two more talents. But the one who had received the

one talent went off and dug a hole in the ground and hid his master's money. After a long time the master of those slaves came and settled accounts with them. Then the one who had received the five talents came forward, bringing five more talents, saying, "Master, you handed over to me five talents; see, I have made five more talents." His master said to him, "Well done, good and trustworthy slave; you have been trustworthy in a few things, I will put you in charge of many things; enter into the joy of your master." And the one with the two talents also came forward, saying, "Master, you handed over to me two talents; see, I have made two more talents." The master said to him, "Well done, good and trustworthy slave; you have been trustworthy in a few things, I will put you in charge of many things; enter into the joy of your master." Then the one who had received the one talent also came forward, saying, "Master, I knew that you were a harsh man, reaping where you did not sow, and gathering where you did not scatter seed; so I was afraid, and I went and hid your talent in the ground. Here you have what is yours." But his master replied, "You wicked and lazy slave! You knew, did you, that I reap where I did not sow, and gather where I did not scatter? Then you ought to have invested my money with the bankers, and on my return I would have received what was my own with interest. So take the talent from him, and give it to the one with the ten talents. . . . As for this worthless slave, throw him into the outer darkness, where there will be weeping and gnashing of teeth." (Matthew 25:14-28, 30, emphasis added)

The last slave did not have a willing heart. He was not willing to take risks for the sake of his master with what his master had entrusted to him. Why? He had a wrong picture of his master. He saw his master as a harsh and judgmental man. He did not see that what the master had entrusted to him represented an opportunity not a threat, and most importantly, *an opportunity that fit his abilities.*

DISTORTED IMAGES OF GOD

The willingness of a disciple to take risks for God with what God has entrusted to her or him can also be diminished to zero by a distorted image of God. God as uncompromising judge, God as stern taskmaster, God as the epitome of harshness—such images of God can close a would-be disciple down.

God as love and justice; God as compassion and mercy; God as calling, enabling, empowering; God as transforming Spirit—such images of God will lead to productive personal growth, powerful ministry to others, and joy.

God as love and justice; God as compassion and mercy; God as calling, enabling, empowering; God as transforming Spirit—such images of God will lead to productive personal growth, powerful ministry to others, and joy. Such images of God are what motivate my friend, the business man, to grasp opportunities that serve the purposes of God.

Unfortunately, all too many people have negative images of God. When they imagine God their picture is often distorted by negative experiences with others that they project onto God—in particular, negative experiences with others in authority.

"I can't pray anymore," she said. "I don't like it, but every time I close my eyes to pray, the picture I see is of my father—angry and abusive."

I listened as this fine woman began to share with me how, through counseling, she was facing her past. After decades of repressing her early childhood, the memories had come flooding out when she began struggling with whether or not to divorce her husband.

The prospect of divorce was the trigger that released the memories of a small girl facing an alcoholic father whom her mother would finally divorce. That divorce eventually led to her mother's remarriage and a healthy family life. And now facing her own decaying marriage, she had begun contemplating divorce—and the memories surfaced.

For the first time in her adult life she struggled with prayer. Whenever she thought of God, the picture of an angry man came to her mind. This was not the God she wanted; this was not the God that she had come to believe in when, as an adult Christian, she had returned to the church.

"You've got to fire that god," I gently asserted. "Unless you fire that god you will not be able to discover the God who alone is God—the God we know in Jesus Christ."

"But how do I do that?" she asked.

"Would you be willing to try an experiment?" I asked. When she nodded her head, I asked if she would join me in prayer. We bowed our heads and closed our eyes. Then I asked her to begin to pray as she always did. When she started, her eyes flew open and she said, "I see that picture all over again!"

One again I asked her to close her eyes and pray. "This time," when you see that picture, "I want you to say, 'In the name of Jesus, you're fired.' If it helps," I continued smiling, "you can picture yourself as Donald Trump in the boardroom."

Once again she closed her eyes and prayed. Then, breathing more quickly, she said, "In the name of Jesus, you're fired." "Say it louder," I said, "as if you mean it."

"You're fired!" she shouted.

"Now," I said, "I want you to picture Jesus standing before you. See his gentle smile. Know that he is here to heal and help you make the difficult decisions you need to make. Know that you can pray to him anytime, anywhere."

It took practice, but that woman fired her wrong picture of God and replaced it with the picture of the Messiah, Jesus.

No matter how willing the heart is, if our picture of God is wrong, the willing heart closes. Sometimes the distorted picture of God comes from our early memories of angry parents who stood like gods before us as children. That was the tragic picture of god that this woman had. It is not unlike the picture that the unworthy slave had of his master in Jesus' story. The consequence was that he reacted in fear and distrust and protected himself by covering up what he had been given.

> God often works the greatest wonders *through* our difficulties—not by simply taking them away.

What could such an image of God have in common with Jesus who, scolding the adults who tried to protect him from the distractions of children, took the children in his arms, loved and blessed them? If Jesus is the self-disclosure of God—and he is—then images of God as an angry parent are false images of God; they are images of God that prevent us from truly knowing and experiencing God.

There are other pictures of God that will get in our way as well. Recognizing that caricature can often open us to truth. Let me highlight a few of them.

Some of us have an image of God as a miracle worker. God is supposed to answer our prayers and rescue us from our problems and hardships. When that "rescuer" god doesn't show up on time, our hearts close in anger and pain. Yet, as we have previously seen, God often works the greatest wonders *through* our difficulties—not by simply taking them away.

Still others picture God as a kindly old man, wise and accepting but somehow distant and powerless. The willing heart of the disciple will not trust such a god when the stakes are high and the pain is great.

Some picture God as a coach, roaming the side line of life with a cosmic clipboard in his hand. His job is to catch us doing wrong, running the wrong play, or making a mistake. Such a relentless god praises little, scolds much, and ultimately takes us out of the game entirely. Such a perfectionist god will naturally threaten and shut down the willing heart. But such a god has nothing to do with the God of the New Testament who, in speaking to that perfectionist Paul, declared, "My strength is made perfect in your weakness."

> When we are willing to open our hearts to God's leading and grow in grace, we discover more fully who we are and what we are capable of accomplishing.

The wrong picture of God not only robs us of a real relationship with the real God; it also shuts us off from our own power. We withdraw from that eternal reservoir that is God's love and close the heart to the assets we already have, let alone those we could receive if we were open to the calling and gifts of God. The tragedy in the parable of the talents is not simply that the frightened slave lost what he had but that his picture of the master was so tragically distorted that he actually received the very thing he feared the most—the judgment of the master.

That's the way it is with all of our false images of God—they distort reality. The way we experience God is shaped by our image of God. If your image of God is that of an angry parent, that's exactly how you will experience God. False images equal false experiences. It is critical, then, that our images of God match the God that Jesus revealed through his teaching, the way he lived, and the way he died. Hence the importance of practicing the *Marks of Discipleship*.

The call to discipleship is a call to radical openness to the being of God; it is an invitation to mystery and identity. As we grow in our knowledge of the God of the Bible, we will discover the wondrous mystery of God's presence meeting us again and again in surprising ways. As we trust in the God of the Scriptures, we open ourselves to the Spirit's actions both within ourselves and in the world.

Perhaps the greatest mystery of God is that, when we are willing to open our hearts to God's leading and grow in grace, we discover more fully who we are and what we are capable of accomplishing. That's what my Christian businessman friend has learned. If you asked him, he would tell you he never thought such accomplishments were possible in his life. This twenty-first century follower of Jesus discovered the truth of what Jesus told his first followers: "For God, all things are possible" (Mark 10:27b).

Don't let anything get in the way of your growing spiritual life—especially a distorted picture of God.

FRUSTRATION

Another block to our progress in growing as disciples is frustration. Very often we begin practicing our faith with expectations that are unreasonable. Spiritual growth is cumulative. Our times of prayer begin to inform our scripture reading and our scripture reading shapes our prayer. Our time in the Bible begins to shape our relationships and how we experience worship. Our deepening relationships and our experience of worship encourages us to keep on reading God's word. One thing builds upon another. When all of the *Marks of Discipleship* are integrated into a disciple's life, the cumulative effect is remarkable growth—and joy. Such "soul construction" takes time and effort. One day you feel as if you haven't grown at all. The next day you are surprised by a spiritual gift, a new insight, a more faithful response to the challenges and opportunities God places before you, and you realize that you are indeed changing; the promise of God is being realized—you are being transformed into Christ-likeness (2 Corinthians 3:18).

Recently I found myself changed through an experience of grace.

"Oh, I don't want to lose him!" my colleague said. "He's been such a good committee chair that I can't imagine being as effective in ministry without his leadership."

"I hope he doesn't leave either," I said, "but what I have learned over time is that when a person leaves the congregation, if we trust God, God will bring us another person—or persons—with the gifts we need. We work to keep people involved, but if for some reason they leave we have to trust the Holy Spirit to provide."

There was a time, not so long ago, when I would have been caught up in the anxiety of my colleague. Once, when I heard that a family was considering leaving the congregation, I made two or three house calls to try to get them to stay. They left anyway. They weren't angry. They simply had very good reasons to move to another congregation: that's where their grandchildren were!

When they left our congregation, they took a very large annual donation with them. But in a manner of months, the Holy Spirit provided two new families that brought renewed leadership and made up for the annual contribution we had lost.

Disciples trust. When I had that brief exchange with my colleague, it was the Holy Spirit that whispered this truth of faith to me and I was confident—not anxious.

Such is the power of spiritual lessons learned through experience by a willing heart. Experiences of God's grace and truth always bring us back to God with renewed confidence in the promises of God.

I've found that my confidence in the promises of God usually grows in three stages. First, I often initially (and understandably) respond to difficult or challenging situations with anxiety. My anxiety leads me to try and control the situation, but my attempts to control the situation rarely lead to the results I hoped for. Such consecutive stages in spiritual growth take time, but the disciple's joy that accompanies such growth is well worth the effort. Frustration sets in. Then (second stage) in the midst of my anxiety and frustration, the Holy Spirit reminds me of similar experiences in the past while also reminding me that, on those occasions when I let go and let God, things had a way of working out. Then I apply that lesson in faith to the situation at hand. It often takes a number of "applications" before I reach stage three.

I know I have reached stage three when I have integrated this faith lesson into my life well enough so that when anxiety causing situations arise I find myself immediately relying on (and trusting) the Holy Spirit instead of reacting in anxiety induced attempts to control things. Such consecutive stages in spiritual growth take time, but the disciple's joy that accompanies such growth is well worth the effort.

Our frustrations can block our spiritual practices. Usually these frustrations are the result of unfounded expectations. We commonly expect to make progress much more quickly than is reasonable. Even though it is impossible, many of us expect ourselves to do things perfectly which only leads to more frustration. What is perfect prayer, perfect Bible study, perfect worship, perfect relationships, perfect generosity, perfect service anyway?

Perfection can be our intent—but it will never leave us content because we will never achieve it! To be human means that we will *grow* in faith and spirituality throughout this life and even into eternity. Growth presumes lack of perfection.

When you feel frustrated with your progress as a disciple, ask yourself if you are expecting to be somewhere you haven't yet reached in your practice of discipleship. Then take heart by reading the Gospel of Mark. As Mark tells it, the first followers of Jesus were anything but perfect! They simply didn't get most of what Jesus was teaching and modeling. They were—like all humans—imperfect people.

Here is but one of many stories that Mark tells which sheds light on the imperfections and failures of Jesus' earliest disciples:

> Then they came to Capernaum; and when he was in the house he asked them, "What were you arguing about on the way?" But they were silent, for on the way they had argued with one another who was the greatest. He sat down, called the twelve, and said to them, "Whoever wants to be first must be last of all and servant of all." (Mark 9:33-35)

They simply didn't get it! Jesus was among them as "one who serves" (Luke 22:27) but they missed the point: *as his followers they too were to be people who served.* Rather than service, they were interested in pride of place, position, power. We can imagine them arguing on the road, caught up in visions of privilege, totally oblivious to what Jesus was trying to teach them.

The point is that the earliest disciples were not perfect and neither are we. In the resurrection power of Jesus, they did great things—not perfect things but great things—and so can we if we don't allow perfectionism to get in the way of truly opening our hearts to all God has for us and wants from us.

Jesus offers us a real faith for our real lives. Jesus invites each of us into a living relationship with God in the power of the Holy Spirit. Real people are not perfect people. In fact, the only severe criticisms Jesus gives are against those who seem to have the crazy idea that they were religiously perfect in the practice of their faith.

> We need to be reminded that neither our faith nor our spirituality can control the Holy Spirit. Outcomes are the Spirit's responsiblity, not ours.

When we get frustrated, let us pray and simply ask God to *continue* growing our faith—and show us that it is growing.

SELF-DEFINED OUTCOMES

One of the temptations disciples of Jesus face is an addiction to *self-defined* outcomes. As we continue to grow in faith and understanding we can easily begin to think that our developing faith will produce the outcomes we hope for. We need to be reminded that neither our faith nor our spirituality can control the Holy Spirit. Outcomes are the Spirit's responsibility, not ours. The Spirit, as Jesus teaches, cannot be domesticated and is not predictable, let alone controllable: "Do not be astonished that I said to you, 'You must be born from above.' The wind blows where it chooses, and you hear the sound of it, but you do not know where it comes from or where it goes. So it is with everyone who is born of the Spirit" (John 3:7-8).

The spiritual disciplines of discipleship are simply tools to empower us to grow spiritually. They are not guarantees. If they were it would defeat their very purpose—to empower us to greater trust in God! Addiction to the outcomes of our practices will lead to frustrations and block our willing hearts. It happens all the time. The antidote is trust.

DISTRACTIONS

Distractions are plentiful in our lives. As I write these words I have a CD on. The music is non-intrusive, but with a change of movement or beat, it could claim my attention. When I drive my car, I usually have the radio on. My cell phone travels with me. When I am at home, I often have the television on or am on the telephone. This, along with simply living in a noisy world, has created in me a certain comfort with noise. But with the noise comes a certain numbing of our awareness.

I believe that most of us feel comfortable when surrounded by noise and are usually not even aware of its numbing effect on our awareness. You can also see it in our children (and in adults). So many walk through life plugged into CD players, IPODS, and cell phones somewhat oblivious to what's going on around them.

In most circumstances, this phenomenon is relatively benign. But spiritual growth requires silence. As God declares through the ancient psalmist: "Be still and know that I am God" (Psalm 46:10).

It is in the quiet of our time with God that we hear the Spirit most clearly. It is in the quiet of our Bible reading, meditation, prayer, and the planned silence in worship that we most frequently hear our own thoughts in the light of faith and can correct or affirm them. Only as we become comfortable with silence can we discern "noise" from "signal."

Noise in our hearts and minds is just that—sounds of nonsense and distortion that block us from hearing what we need to hear. Without silence we cannot listen for and learn the many truths that God would teach us. Without silence we cannot separate the signal of spiritual growth from the noise of all the other messages within and outside of ourselves that can drown out God's invitation to inner confidence, strength, significance, purpose, and joy.

Lately I have found myself reaching over and turning the car radio or CD off. I am not sure when it began. I cannot remember a time when I made the decision to do so. Instead it has simply happened with greater frequency in my life lately. The pleasure of reflection, the prayers said in the midst of traffic, and the resulting slowing of my pulse as well as my rate of travel have been significant. And I find that I am quite simply more present when I arrive at my destination.

> The invitation to silence that emerges from practicing our discipleship is to a deeper level of presence to all of life and to all that would meet us in life—especially God.

I have no idea if those around me experience my presence as different since I started spending more time in silence. It doesn't matter. I do. Silence enables me to be less distracted, more present to others, and more loving. I find that I am able to listen undistractedly and participate at a different, more effective, and more faithful level.

Noise, whether internal or external, separates us from God, ourselves, and one another. The noise of life can create dissonance within that can separate us from the best of who we are. But it can also intrude between spouses, parents and children, good friends, colleagues, and others. My internal noise can keep me from truly hearing another person (or God). External noise can literally make it impossible for me to hear what another person (or God) is saying. The problem is that I (along with just about everyone else) have grown accustomed to noise. The antidote is deliberately making room for times of silence in our fast paced, busy, and noisy world.

The invitation to silence that emerges from practicing our discipleship is to a deeper level of presence to all of life and to all that would meet us in life—especially God. The invitation to silence is one of God's many invitations to joy.

A MATTER OF PRIORITIES

"Ministry and life are all about priorities," Bishop Cliff Lunde told me. "The important thing is that we know what our priorities are so that we can identify what really matters to us. The problem is that if you have more than three priorities, you don't have priorities at all. You've just got a list."

Bishop Lunde has joined his wonderful wife, Jillian, in eternity, but this was one of the gems of wisdom he left for me. His point is that distractions are a part of life, but if we understand what truly matters, we can manage the distractions because we know, ultimately, how we have chosen to live, how we have chosen to give ourselves to a life of significance and purpose.

The decision to practice our faith by committing to the *Marks of Discipleship* empowers us. As we strive to live our faith and grow in God's grace and guidance, our priorities become aligned with the love we receive in Jesus the Savior. And therein is the disciple's joy.

Not long ago, a pastor challenged me. "Mike," he asked, "what if people practice the *Marks of Discipleship* for the wrong reasons? What if they do the '*Marks*' as an attempt to become spiritually superior?"

"I don't care," I replied. "I'm not being flippant," I continued. "I just don't care what the motivation is. Let me ask you a question. Do you really believe that anyone can grow closer to Jesus Christ and remain unchanged? I don't. I have watched the Holy Spirit transform the lives of people who I didn't think could ever be changed. The *Marks of Discipleship* are nothing more than tried and true biblical and historical practices of faith. I am confident that the Holy Spirit will have his way with anyone who practices them over time—and their priorities will change."

The power of God to transform us and our world that is released through prayer, worship, Bible reading, serving, relating spiritually, and tithing is enormous. In each of the practices we place ourselves consciously in the presence and power of the Holy Spirit. This will necessarily transform how we understand whatever happens in our lives. Practicing the *Marks of Discipleship* will inevitably turn our lives toward the priorities of faith. Those priorities will, over time, empower us to differentiate distractions from necessities, good things from important things.

As Jim Collins, author of *Good to Great* (2001), has said, "Good is the enemy of best." And he is right. Only God can, over time, open our lives to the best and empower us to stop cluttering our lives with the merely good.

God calls us to the best—and when we answer the call, the outcome is always joy. The journey of life is God's invitation to joy. Don't let anything get in the way of your discovering all that God wants for you and from you.

QUESTIONS FOR FURTHER REFLECTION

❦ Have you started practicing the *Marks of Discipleship* yet? If not, what's preventing you? If you have, how's it going?

❦ What opportunities has God presented to you for service that you have grasped? Any opportunities you have not grasped? If so, why?

❦ Would you say you do or don't have a "willing heart?" Explain your answer. If you find more willfulness than willingness in your heart, what might you do about it?

❦ Are you happy with your spiritual growth? If not, what might be getting in your way?

❦ In what ways do you trust God? In what ways is trust difficult for you?

❦ How do you use silence for spiritual growth? Where do you find silence in your life? Are there any ways you could increase silence in your life?

References

Beecher, H. W. In Wallace C., ed. *The Treasure Chest.* San Francisco: Harper and Row. 1983. 159.

Bibesco, E. In Wallace C., ed. *The Treasure Chest.* San Francisco: Harper and Row. 1983. 103.

Brayne, et al. "Deathbed Phenomena and Their Effect On A Palliative Care Team: Pilot Study." *America Journal of Hospital Palliative Care.* 32:1, 2006. 17–24.

Collins, J. *Good to Great.* New York: Random House. 2001.

Consedine N. S., et al. "Deconstructing Positive Affect in Later Life: A Differential Functionalist Analysis of Joy and Interest." *International Journal of Aging and Human Development.* 2004. 49–68.

Easterbrook, G. *The Progress Paradox.* New York: Random House. 2004. 180

Gillum R. F., Ingram D. D. "Frequency of Attendance at Religious Services, Hypertension, and Blood Pressure." *Psychosomatic Medicine* 68:3, 2006. 382–385.

Hall, A. C. In Wallace C., ed. *The Treasure Chest.* San Francisco: Harper and Row. 1983. 159.

Keller, H. In Wallace C., ed. *The Treasure Chest.* San Francisco: Harper and Row. 1983. 57.

Lewis, T., Amini, F., Lannon, R. *A General Theory of Love.* New York: Vintage. 2001.

Morris E. L. "The Relationship of Spirituality to Coronary Heart Disease." *Alternative Therapy Health and Medicine.* 7:5, 2001. 96–98.

Washington, B. T. In Wallace C., ed. *The Treasure Chest.* San Francisco: Harper and Row. 1983. 1.

Wilson, E. In Easterbrook, G. *The Progress Paradox.* New York: Random House. 2004. 177, 179.